Orlando

Text by John Gattuso
Principal photographer: Richard Nowitz
Cover photograph: Courtesy Busch Gardens
Layout Concept: Klaus Geisler
Managing Editor: Tony Halliday

Berlitz POCKET GUIDE

Orlando

First Edition 2003

Additional photography by:
6, 12, 13 courtesy Library of Congress; 15 courtesy Orange County Regional History Center; 29, 30 courtesy Everett Collection; 52 courtesy Universal Orlando; 74/75 courtesy Mennello Museum of American Folk Art; 94 courtesy Orlando Magic.

CONTACTING THE EDITORS

Every effort has been made to provide accurate information in this publication, but changes are inevitable. The publisher cannot be responsible for any resulting loss, inconvenience or injury. We would appreciate it if readers would call our attention to any errors or outdated information by contacting Berlitz Publishing, PO Box 7910, London SE1 1WE, England.
Fax: (44) 20 7403 0290;
e-mail: berlitz@apaguide.co.uk
www.berlitzpublishing.com

917.59240
0712

▶ Downtown Disney encompasses restaurants, stores and an adults-only nightclub district (page 35)

The Orlando Science Center is one of three top-flight museums in Loch Haven Park (page 73) ▲

Gatorland is one of the few roadside attractions that have survived the Disney age (page 68) ▼

TOP TEN ATTRACTIONS

The Muppets and other familiar characters appear at Disney-MGM Studios (page 27)

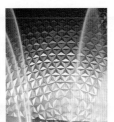

Spaceship Earth rises over Epcot, designed as a permanent World's Fair (page 24)

Animal Kingdom, Walt Disney World's newest and largest theme park, features naturalistic enclosures inhabited by hundreds of wild creatures (page 32)

Guests at Discovery Cove, SeaWorld's new all-inclusive park, swim with dolphins (page 65)

The Incredible Hulk Coaster rockets over Islands of Adventure, Universal Orlando's latest theme park (page 47)

Movie magic comes to life at Universal Studios (page 39)

The Hard Rock Cafe is one of a dozen restaurants and nightclubs at CityWalk, Universal's nighttime entertainment complex (page 55)

CONTENTS

Fact Sheets

INTRODUCTION

Of Walt Disney's many accomplishments, perhaps the most enduring is the transformation of an obscure Florida town into America's most visited tourist destination. The Orlando metro area, home of Walt Disney World, attracts more than 43 million travelers a year – nearly three times the population of Florida itself. Disney World gets the lion's share of tourist dollars, of course, but it no longer has the monopoly it once did. Universal Orlando, which now encompasses two major theme parks, three hotels, and an entertainment district, has nibbled away at Mickey's market share, as has SeaWorld and its new all-inclusive resort, Discovery Cove. There are hundreds of hotels, restaurants, and small-scale attractions, too, which means that Disney may be the biggest mouse in town, but it's not the only one.

Not Just for Kids

Orlando isn't strictly for families with young children. As the city has matured, so too has its appeal to adults. Even Disney World – originally conceived as a 'timeless land of enchantment' – has made an effort to cater to grownup tastes, with fine restaurants, first-class spas, a professional sports facility, even a nightclub district where the over-21 crowd can booze and schmooze into the wee hours. Universal followed suit by opening its own entertainment complex, dubbed City-Walk, which has restaurants and nightclubs that keep rocking well after the kiddies are tucked into bed.

> **Walt Disney initially wanted to name his famous cartoon mouse Mortimer. Walt's wife Lillian thought the name stuffy and suggested Mickey instead. The name stuck, and a star was born.**

Lest you think Orlando is all kitsch and no culture, consider that the area has some of the state's finest museums, more than a dozen venues for the performing arts, a philharmonic orchestra, ballet and opera companies, and several independent theater groups, as well as lush botanical gardens and wilderness preserves. There's also been something of a restaurant renaissance in town, as a generation of savvy young chefs and entrepreneurs lead the way out of Orlando's fast-food wasteland. Even Disney World, long criticized for its lackluster performance in the kitchen, has made strides toward improving the overall quality of its food service.

Making the Most of Your Visit

The first thing you should know about a holiday in Orlando is that this is not the sort of place that rewards spontaneity. Planning is essential, and reservations – for hotels, rental cars, and restaurants – are a must.

Timing is equally important. The two biggest gripes tourists have about Orlando are the crowds and the prices. You can minimize both by traveling off-season, when the theme parks aren't quite so mobbed and hotels and airlines offer sizable discounts. The period between Thanksgiving and Christmas is the least crowded, though the weather can be chilly. Fall, from

---

Life in the fast lane

Both Disney and Universal have instituted programs to reduce waiting times at their most popular attractions. Disney calls it Fastpass, Universal calls it Universal Express, but they work basically the same way. You insert your ticket into an electronic kiosk near the entrance of the ride, select a time to return, and get a chit that serves as an express ticket. When you come back, you're whisked to the front of the line, cutting your queue time by half, if not more.

Dueling Dragons roller coaster at Universal's Islands of Adventure

mid-September to mid-November, is better as far as weather is concerned, and the crowds are usually manageable on week-days. While those dates are difficult for folks with school-age children, they're ideal for travelers without kids.

Time of day is a consideration, too. In general, attendance at theme parks peaks between the hours of 11am and 4pm. The best strategy, therefore, is to arrive as early as possible, take a break in the afternoon for shopping and a sit-down meal (or, if you're staying at an on-site resort, sneak back to your hotel for a snooze and a swim), then pick up the trail in the late afternoon or evening.

Keep in mind that the gates at Disney World and Universal usually open 30 to 60 minutes earlier than the scheduled times. Granted, dragging yourself out of bed at 7am in order to get to the Magic Kingdom by 8am hardly sounds like a vacation, but you can often do more in the first couple of hours of the day, when lines are short, temperatures are mild, and you're feeling fresh, than in the remainder of the afternoon.

Attitude is a key element, too. Resist the temptation to be overly ambitious. The tendency among many visitors is to squeeze as much as possible into the shortest period of time, frantically trying to get their money's worth. But before you commit yourself to an elaborate touring plan, consider the hazards of trying to do too much. Unrealistic expectations will lead only to disappointment and exhaustion. Unless you enjoy running frantically from one attraction to another, forget about cramming everything into a short visit or even following some preordained schedule. Instead, select three or four 'must-dos' for each day and fill in with other attractions as time allows.

Remember, you're on vacation. If you find yourself feeling more stressed-out than on a typical day at work, you're probably missing the point.

Splashdown on Journey to Atlantis, a water ride at SeaWorld

A BRIEF HISTORY

When Walt Disney arrived in 1963, Orlando was a modest city surrounded by orange groves, cattle ranches, and swampland. Though it seemed a peaceful, out-of-the-way place, the region had been buffeted by world events for centuries.

Before Europeans appeared on the scene, central Florida was the domain of the Timucua Indians, a large and powerful tribe known for elaborate temple mounds, ornate body art, and ferocity in battle. Though Juan Ponce de León claimed Florida for Spain in 1513, neither he nor conquistador Hernando de Soto were able to subdue the Indians well enough to establish a settlement. De León returned to Florida in 1521 but was repelled yet again, this time fatally. Wounded by an arrow, he sailed back to Cuba and soon died.

The French, who were generally more interested in trade than conquest, had better luck – at least initially. A French party led by René de Laudonnière established Fort Caroline near the mouth of the St John's River in 1564, only to be slaughtered a year later by Spanish soldiers under the command of Pedro Menendez de Aviles, who started his own compound at St Augustine, now the oldest city in the United States.

Power Struggle
Predictably, violence begat violence as the Spanish, French, and later the British vied for dominance over the Florida peninsula and the strategic waters between North America and the Caribbean. The French retaliated by attacking an outpost called San Mateo in 1568 and hanging every Spaniard they could get their hands on. The Spanish promptly returned the favor by hunting down the few French stragglers who

Seminoles attacking an American fort, about 1837

remained on the coast. And the British, who were busy planting colonies farther north, engaged in countless skirmishes along the Florida–Georgia border, including an attack in 1586 led by Sir Francis Drake that left St Augustine in ashes.

And so it went for more than two centuries – raid, revenge, and counter-raid – until the United States, feeling its oats after winning the War of 1812, annexed the peninsula from Spain. The man behind the American takeover was Andrew Jackson, a frontier general and politician who had made a name for himself as a war hero, an Indian fighter and a champion of what would later be termed 'manifest destiny.'

Jackson's justification for marching into Florida was to punish Seminole Indians who were raiding settlements along the Florida border. The display of military muscle wasn't lost on Spain. With its treasury depleted and its empire falling down around its ears, the once mighty Iberians reluctantly signed the Adams-Onis treaty of 1819 ceding Florida to the United States.

The Seminoles proved a far more stubborn obstacle. Led by guerilla fighters including Osceola and Billy Bowlegs, they resisted Jackson's policy of Indian removal for more than 20 years, harassing American troops with sudden attacks, then evaporating into the swampy interior. Finally, in 1842, the US government decided that the Seminole War was more trouble than it was worth. In the end, 3,800 Seminoles were shipped west to Indian Territory, about two for every soldier killed in the fighting. A few hundred Seminoles stayed in the swamps, where their descendants remain today.

Florida Frontier

The first American settlers to stake a claim to what would later become Orlando were Aaron and Isaac Jernigan, brothers from Georgia who, in 1843, accepted government grants of 160 acres (65 hectares) in return for military service at Fort Gatlin. Others soon joined them, and by the outbreak of the Civil War the town – initially called Jernigan, later renamed Orlando (most likely for a settler whose homestead was burned down by Seminoles) – was an isolated, rough-hewn settlement of cotton farmers and cattlemen.

Citrus growers moved into the area after the war, aided in 1880 by the arrival of the South Florida Railroad, which provided vital northern connections. A fire devastated downtown Orlando in 1884 and a killer frost wiped out orange groves in 1894. The town soon rebounded and by 1910, with a population of 4,000, it was poised to

Osceola, Seminole leader

become central Florida's transportation hub, business center and, thanks to the invention of the air conditioner, an attractive place to relocate.

The Mouse Has Landed

Then came Walt, and everything changed. In 1963, after scouting sites in Missouri, New York, Maryland, and Ocala, Florida, Walt selected Orlando for the location of his new theme park. The area had much to recommend it: balmy weather, good roads, two airports and, most important, plenty of room to grow. Unlike Walt's first park, Disneyland in California, this

Welcome to Waltopia

Walt Disney originally conceived of Epcot as a living laboratory – an Experimental Prototype Community of Tomorrow (EPCOT) that would blaze a trail into a brave new world of urban design and technology. It was to be a modern utopia built 'from scratch on virgin land' and contained beneath a glass dome. The industrial center was to be surrounded by a ring of suburban housing and connected to it by monorail. 'The pedestrian will be king,' said Walt in a promotional film made shortly before his death. Automobiles were to be relegated to underground tunnels.

But Walt's utopia also had an authoritarian side. 'In Epcot there will be no slum areas,' he declared, 'because we won't let them develop'. And presumably the 20,000 residents would waive their rights to vote and own property: 'There will be no landowners and therefore no voting control. People will rent houses instead of buying them'. Slackers – even retirees – were not welcome: 'everyone must be employed.' Alas, the vision perished with its creator. After Walt passed away in 1966, park planners reconfigured the concept along commercial lines, transforming his pie-in-the-sky city into a marketable product – the Epcot we know today.

new property was intended to be a self-contained resort designed to keep visitors (and their money) on-site for several days.

Land acquisition began immediately and in the utmost secrecy in order to prevent speculators from driving up prices. In the end, Walt's agents cobbled together 27,300 acres (11,000 hectares), an area comparable in size to the city of Boston.

Walt and Roy Disney announce plans for a new theme park

And for all practical purposes, the project Walt had in mind *was* a city. It was to have its own police, fire, and sanitation departments as well as its own power plant and water treatment facility. It was also granted quasi-governmental status, thanks to a deal that Walt and brother Roy cut with the state of Florida creating the Reedy Creek Improvement District, a 'public corporation' that endowed Disney with such municipal powers as issuing bonds, levying taxes, writing building codes, and even building an airport or a nuclear power plant should the need arise.

Construction of the park took more than three years and cost $400 million. Sadly, Walt never saw the fulfillment of his dream. He succumbed to lung cancer in 1966, leaving responsibility for the park's completion in the hands of brother Roy.

The park opened on October 1, 1971, and was a whopping success right off the bat, attracting 20 million visitors in its first two years of operation. Other attractions sprang up like mushrooms. Most were short-lived, although a few, like Sea-World, a marine park owned by Anheuser-Busch, are still major players. This is also the period in which International

Drive was developed – a tourist corridor just outside Disney World lined with restaurants, shops and hotels.

Disney World was expanding, too. Ground broke in 1979 on Epcot, a 'permanent World's Fair' devoted to the themes of international brotherhood and technological progress. It was unveiled in 1982 to wide acclaim and a jump in attendance of 81 percent. Disney-MGM Studios opened in 1989, capitalizing on a string of blockbuster movies produced under the stewardship of CEO Michael Eisner. Typhoon Lagoon, the second of Disney's three water parks, also opened in 1989, as did Pleasure Island, a nightclub district that's now part of Downtown Disney. In 1998, the company christened the *Disney Magic*, the first of two ships in its own cruise line, and launched Animal Kingdom, the largest of Disney World's four theme parks.

A Piece of the Action

Despite its warm and cuddly image, Disney made no bones about targeting competitors. Pleasure Island, for example, was a direct response to Church Street Station, a now-defunct entertainment complex in downtown Orlando. Disney-MGM Studios scooped Universal Studios, Animal Kingdom parried Busch Gardens, and Epcot's forthcoming Mission: Space is Disney's answer to the Kennedy Space Center.

While the Mouse has no rivals of comparable size, one company – Universal – has managed to put a dent in its market share. Following up on the success of Universal Studios, which opened in Orlando in 1990, the company poured more than a billion dollars into the construction of a second park, the elaborately themed Islands of Adventure, and an adjoining entertainment district called CityWalk. The completion of three hotels, including the high-profile Hard Rock Hotel, completed Universal's transformation into a self-contained, multiday resort similar to Disney World, albeit on a much smaller scale.

Historical Landmarks

AD **15–mid-1500s** Timucua Indians occupy central Florida.

1513 Ponce de León lands near what is now Cape Canaveral, claims the territory for Spain and names it La Florida. He returns in 1521 and is fatally wounded by an Indian arrow.

1528 In separate journeys, Panfilo de Navaez and Hernando de Soto fail to colonize the Tampa Bay area.

1564–65 French traders build Fort Caroline but are attacked and killed by Spaniard Pedro Menendez de Aviles, who establishes St Augustine.

1586 Sir Francis Drake burns St Augustine.

1740 Georgia founder James Oglethorpe attacks Florida settlements and lays siege to St Augustine.

Mid-1700s Creek Indians and runaway slaves are driven south into Florida, where they become known as Seminoles.

1764–83 Spain is ousted from Florida by Britain, then reinstated by the US after the American Revolution.

1813 Andrew Jackson attacks Seminoles and captures Pensacola, prompting Spain to cede Florida to the US.

1818–43 Seminole Wars result in the deaths of more than 1,500 Americans and removal of 3,800 Seminoles.

1843 Jernigan brothers settle in Orlando area.

1894–99 Severe frost wipes out Orlando citrus groves.

1964 The Disney Company secretly buys land around Orlando.

1966 Walt Disney dies.

1971 The Magic Kingdom opens.

1973 SeaWorld Orlando opens.

1982 Epcot opens.

1989 Disney-MGM Studios opens.

1990 Universal Studios opens in Orlando.

1998 Disney unveils Animal Kingdom and cruise line.

1999 Universal opens Islands of Adventure and CityWalk.

2001 9/11 terrorist attacks cause a sharp downturn in tourism. Theme park attendance suffers.

WHERE TO GO

Finding your way around the Orlando area is a snap. The hot spots for tourists are strung along a 20-mile (32-km) stretch of I-40 that runs from downtown Orlando through Walt Disney World. In between are Universal Orlando, SeaWorld, the Holyland Experience, the Orlando-Orange County Convention Center, and a bevy of attractions on International Drive. Kissimmee, a popular gateway to Disney World with hotels, restaurants, and quite a few attractions of its own, is about 5 miles (8km) southeast of Disney World via US 192, also known as the Irlo Bronson Memorial Highway. Orlando International Airport is about 16 miles (26km) northeast of Disney World and 10 miles (16km) southeast of downtown Orlando.

WALT DISNEY WORLD

Even if you're not enthralled by the Disney mystique, it's virtually impossible to walk away from Disney World without an appreciation for the magnitude of the endeavor, the artistry of the Disney 'imagineers' and the logistical complexities of keeping the place up and running.

Encompassed within Disney's World's 43 sq miles (111 sq km) – an area twice the size of Manhattan – are four of the most elaborate theme parks ever constructed, three water parks, two entertainment districts, six golf courses, three spas, and more than 15 hotels and 100 restaurants. While nearly everything is suitable for families, there's no lack of grown-up pleasures. Indeed, some people come back year after year – with or without children – and never feel they've seen and done it all.

Magic Kingdom

The Magic Kingdom is Disney World's oldest park and the one closest to Walt's original vision of a 'timeless land of

Magic Kingdom visitor

enchantment.' Not coincidentally, it's also the place that has the least to offer adults. This is, at heart, a children's park – beautifully designed but intended for wholesome, innocent fun. That's fine if you're in a nostalgic mood. But if you're pursuing a mature agenda – wine, candlelight, romance, that sort of thing – you're in the wrong place. There's no alcohol at the Magic Kingdom, precious little fine dining, and nothing more risqué than the Little Mermaid's bikini.

Main Street to the Old West

Setting the stage at the entrance to the park is Main Street, USA, a picture-perfect evocation of an American town. Although there are no rides or shows here, there are more than a dozen stores and restaurants as well as a fleet of double-decker buses, horse-drawn trolleys, and old-fashioned fire trucks. At the top of Main Street, housed in a stately Victorian-style building near the entrance, is the **Walt Disney World Railroad**, which takes passengers on a 20-minute circuit around the park in vintage steam engines.

Main Street leads to a roundabout known as the **Hub**, beyond which is **Cinderella's Castle**, the visual anchor of the park and a Disney icon second only to Mickey himself. Pathways radiate from this central plaza into five distinct 'lands,' starting on the left (as you face Cinderella's Castle) with **Adventureland**, a mélange of fantasy architecture and lush plantings meant to evoke such exotic locales as the South Seas and the Amazon. The attractions here are a mixed bag for adults. **Pirates of the Caribbean** is the best of the lot – an audio-animatronic romp through the Spanish Main with rum-swilling buccaneers and lots of yo-ho-ho high spirits. The other attractions – **Swiss Family Treehouse**, **Jungle Cruise**, and **Enchanted Tiki Room** – are classic Disney. Check them out if lines are short; otherwise, stroll over to **Frontierland**, where the theme is the Old West and the rides are more interesting.

The two biggies at Frontierland are **Splash Mountain** and **Big Thunder Mountain Railroad**. The first is a log flume ride with a *Song of the South* theme and a drenching, five-story finale – enough to elicit screams without inducing real terror. The other is a roller coaster in an elaborate red-rock setting. Scenes of ramshackle mining camps whiz by as your runaway train careens through canyons and caverns and over rickety bridges. Though this is hardly a kiddie ride, it's a piece of cake compared to the big coasters at other Orlando parks.

Another big attraction in Frontierland is the **Country Bear Jamboree** – a 16-minute hillbilly revue starring a cast of animatronic bears. Though it's been a crowd-pleaser for nearly three decades, the cornpone humor isn't everybody's cup of tea. Same goes for the **Diamond Horseshoe Saloon Revue**, a live stage show with can-can girls and a changing

---

Driving Ambition

Ever wanted to get behind the wheel of a stock car? Here's your chance. The Richard Petty Driving Experience puts you in a 600-horsepower race car and lets you zoom around the Walt Disney World Speedway at 145 mph (235kph). Participants have several options: You can do a few laps with a professional driver for about $95 or learn how to drive yourself for $370–$1,270, depending on the program's length. The speedway is near the Magic Kingdom, adjacent to the Transportation and Ticket Center; for information, call (800) 237-3889.

All smiles at Liberty Square

roster of magicians, musicians and jokesters.

Ghosts and Presidents

The Wild West melds into colonial America in **Liberty Square**. The most popular attraction here – and perhaps the best in the park – is the **Haunted Mansion**. Visitors board a 'doom buggy' for a tour of the house, visiting a library full of 'ghost writers,' a haunted ballroom, and, in a clever bit of 'astral projection,' an apparition that appears in your car. The holographic effects – cutting edge when the ride opened some 25 years ago – still hold up pretty well.

On the opposite side of Liberty Square, the **Hall of Presidents** is an animatronic show with a true-blue American theme. The high point is a roll call of all 43 US presidents, followed by remarks from George W. Bush and Abraham Lincoln.

The next two areas, **Fantasyland** and **Mickey's Toontown Fair**, are intended for the preschool crowd. Kiddie rides such as Dumbo the Flying Elephant and Cinderella's Golden Carousel will be familiar to anyone who has been to a county fair, although Disney dresses them up beautifully. Notable among them is **'It's a small world'**, the ride that Disney critics love to hate, featuring scores of animatronic dolls in folksy costumes singing a chirpy melody. Love it or hate it, you can't say you've experienced the Magic Kingdom without riding at least once.

If you have time for only one other attraction here, it should be **Legend of the Lion King**, a live show featuring huge puppets, film, and a variety of special effects.

Tomorrow's World

Wrap up your visit to the Magic Kingdom at **Tomorrowland**, a confection of chrome-and-neon architecture inspired by such disparate sources as H.G. Wells and Fritz Lang's *Metropolis*. Several attractions here will appeal to adults. **Space Mountain** is an indoor roller coaster replete with whiz-bang visual effects, including scary stretches of inky darkness. The ride is bumpy enough to rattle your innards without the loop-the-loops of the mega-coasters at other parks. **Buzz Lightyear's Space Ranger Spin** is fun, too – a cross between a dark ride and a shooting arcade that lets you zap 'aliens' with a laser gun while being whisked around an indoor track. At **Walt Disney's Carousel of Progress**, the audience sits in a rotating theater that chronicles the way technology has changed the lives of an animatronic family.

A couple of shows are well worth seeing, both of them heavy on concept and special effects. **The Timekeeper** is a film projected on a 360-degree screen, hosted by a wacky robot voiced by comedian Robin Williams. Just across the walkway is the terrifying **ExtraTERRORestrial Alien Encounter**, a sci-fi scarefest involving an interstellar teleportation device that goes awry. Before you know it, you're in the company of an ill-tempered alien who makes Godzilla look like a puppy dog.

> The day ends at the Magic Kingdom with a fireworks display called Fantasy in the Sky. You'll get good views on Main Street. Even better, plan to have dinner at the California Grill, overlooking the park from the Contemporary Resort's 15th floor.

Epcot

Disney World's second theme park, Epcot, opened in 1982, is modeled loosely on a World's Fair, with an emphasis on education as well as entertainment. The park is laid out in two circular areas. The first, **Future World**, anchored by that monumental silver golf ball called Spaceship Earth, is devoted to science and technology. Its attractions are housed in pavilions that contain rides, shows, and exhibitions sponsored by big corporations.

Housed within **Spaceship Earth** is a dark ride, sponsored by AT&T, that takes passengers through a series of animatronic tableaux chronicling the history of communications from the Stone Age to the Space Age.

To the left of Spaceship Earth (in the outer ring of World Showcase) is **Universe of Energy**, sponsored by Exxon Mobil. The main attraction here, a combination film and dark ride called **Ellen's Energy Adventure**, is a comedic take on the issue of energy use. Plodding and poorly scripted, the 45-minute show isn't worth seeing on your first visit.

> The Tapestry of Dreams is a pageant of dancers, drummers, stiltwalkers, and giant puppets that circles World Showcase twice nightly. The second parade is followed by IllumiNations, a fireworks spectacular with lasers and fountains. Among the most prized vantage points are the terraces at the Rose & Crown Pub and Cantina de San Angel. Arrive early and ask the host for a table with a view.

The Meaning of Life

More promising is the **Wonders of Life**, in the next pavilion. Here you'll find three worthy attractions: **Body Wars**, a simulator ride that sends you on a frenetic journey through the human body (a no-no for those with motion sickness); **Cranium Command**, a multimedia show with several familiar faces (Charles Grodin, Dana Carvey, John Lovitz) that puts you inside the brain of a 12-year-old boy; and *The Making of Me*, a movie starring Martin Short that answers the question, 'Where do babies come from?'

Next to the Wonders of Life are the sweeping contours of **Planetary Plaza**, the welcome center for Epcot's latest attraction, **Mission:**

Spaceship Earth

SPACE. Open in 2003, it promises to deliver an 'astronaut-like' experience, with exhibits that simulate lift-off and the weightlessness of space. Disney even hired NASA consultants to design the ride – a 'flight' to an international space station.

The next attraction, **General Motors Test Track**, features six-person vehicles that undergo a series of 'tests' – acceleration, road handling, suspension, crash – that simulate the course at a GM proving ground. More appealing to kids than adults and often bogged down with long lines, this is another attraction you may want to put off until a second visit.

From the Test Track, it's a short walk to a pair of low-slung buildings that bracket World Showcase's central plaza. This is **Innoventions**, an exposition of new products developed by companies like Motorola and IBM. A perennial favorite is a section devoted to Sega's latest video games. One problem with Innoventions: the coolest gizmos are often monopolized by kids who have little patience for slow-moving adults.

On the opposite flank of World Showcase is a trio of pavilions, each worth a visit given enough time. The centerpiece of **Living Seas** is a huge saltwater aquarium containing an artificial coral reef populated by tropical fish, sharks, sea turtles, and an occasional scuba diver. Dolphins and manatees are given their own tanks where visitors can get a close-up view.

The main attraction next door at **The Land** is a gentle boat ride that transports riders through a simulation of several ecosystems, then into an expansive experimental greenhouse. The two shows in this pavilion, **Food Rocks** and **The Circle of Life**, are well-produced but appeal mostly to kids.

The big draw over at the **Imagination!** pavilion is a 3-D movie, *Honey, I Shrunk the Audience*. The story line is silly, but the effects are amazing. The dark ride in this pavilion, called **Journey into Your Imagination**, is one of Epcot's misfires; skip it your first time around.

Around the World

The other part of Epcot, **World Showcase**, encompasses 11 pavilions arrayed around a 40-acre (16-hectare) lagoon, each representing a different country and featuring live shows,

---

Disney's Hometown

Epcot was originally conceived by Walt Disney as an experiment in urban planning – an Experimental Prototype Community of Tomorrow – but the plan was abandoned after his death in favor of a commercially viable theme park. The idea was revived in 1994 in the form of Celebration, a town designed from the ground up by Disney 'imagineers'. Numbering about 5,000 residents, the town has the manicured look of a theme park, with a spotless downtown and houses designed by some of the most notable architects in the business. But it hasn't all been smooth sailing. Some residents chafed at the restrictive bylaws, and the school ran afoul of parents and county supervisors over its progressive agenda. So, is Disney's experiment in 'new urbanism' a success? Judge for yourself. Celebration is 5 miles (8km) south of Disney World near the intersection of US 192 and I-4. For information, call (407) 566-2200.

splashy films, and restaurants with native food.

You could spend hours wandering from one 'country' to another, browsing, sampling the cuisine, and taking in replicas of buildings like the Doge's Palace and the Eiffel Tower. There are only two rides, neither too exciting. The movies, on the other hand, are quite spectacular. Two films – in China and

IllumiNations over Epcot

Canada – are projected on 360-degree screens. The restaurants at World Showcase are quite good, too. Les Chefs du France is ranked as one of Disney's best, and L'Originale Alfredo di Roma Ristorante and San Angel Inn are worthy runners-up.

Disney-MGM Studios

Dedicated to the 'Hollywood that never was and always will be,' Disney-MGM is, for many adults, Disney World's most satisfying park. An unabashed attempt to compete with Universal Studios, the park combines some of Disney's best shows and thrill rides with a behind-the-scenes look at the art and technology of movie making.

Upon entering the park, visitors are immediately transported back to the golden age of Hollywood. Lining either side of Hollywood Boulevard – the park's main staging area – are replicas of iconic Tinseltown buildings, most housing stores stocked with Disney merchandise. This is also the first place you'll encounter costumed characters, including actors playing stock Hollywood 'types.'

Towering over a plaza at the end of Hollywood Boulevard is a 12-story **Sorcerer's Hat** like the one worn by Mickey Mouse in *Fantasia*. Kiosks beneath the hat review highlights in Disney history – not worth the time if you're on a tight schedule.

Behind the Sorcerer's Hat, in a replica of Graumann's Chinese Theatre, is **The Great Movie Ride**, which promises to take guests on a 'spectacular journey into the movies.' Actually, it's a tram ride through a series of animatronic stage sets – Julie Andrews in *Mary Poppins*, Johnny Weismuller in *Tarzan*, Bergman and Bogey in *Casablanca,* and others.

Hollywood iconography continues on Sunset Boulevard, which veers off to the right of the plaza. About halfway down, in a roofed 1,500-seat amphitheater modeled after the Hollywood Bowl, is **Beauty and the Beast: Live on Stage**, a 30-minute encapsulation of the animated movie, with a live cast singing to a prerecorded track.

All Shook Up

A few steps away is the entrance to a second open-air venue, the Hollywood Hills Amphitheater. This is the site of **Fantasmic**, Disney-MGM's big finale, which plays nightly just before closing. The special-effects crew pulls out all the stops, dazzling the audience with lasers, fountains, and fire balls in a show that pits Mickey Mouse against Disney's nastiest villains.

> **Seating for Fantasmic begins 2 hours before curtain time. You can reduce the wait by arranging a dinner-and-show combo at the Hollywood Brown Derby or Mama Melrose's Ristorante, which entitles you to priority seating at the eateries and the theater.**

The structure at the end of Sunset Boulevard is the **Twilight Zone Tower of Terror**, housed in what appears to be an abandoned hotel. Inside, you're ushered into an 'elevator' that hurtles through space with a few pauses for creepy, heart-stopping views. This is not an experience for those with shaky stomachs or a fear of heights.

The excitement (and nausea) continues over at the **Rock 'n' Roller Coaster Starring Aerosmith**, an indoor coaster that will satisfy hard-core thrill-seekers. The launch is especially riveting, 0–60mph (97kph) in less than 3 seconds. Warning: this is not a ride for lightweights. If you thought Space Mountain was a challenge, this one will knock you for a loop.

Around Echo Lake

Return to the Sorcerer's Hat and explore the area on the opposite side of the plaza around **Echo Lake**. The big draw here is the **Indiana Jones Epic Stunt Spectacular**, starring stuntmen who

Rod Serling welcomes guests to the Tower of Terror

reenact several scenes from *Raiders of the Lost Ark*. There are gunfights, fistfights, and other feats of derring-do, not to mention a couple of searing explosions.

Across the way is ***Sounds Dangerous***, a comedy starring Drew Carey, who plays an undercover reporter on the trail of a smuggler. Most of the show takes place in the dark, while the audience listens in with headphones. The script is silly, but the experience illustrates how sound is used to advance a story.

An Imperial Walker, one of those spacey war machines that sprang from the mind of George Lucas, stands in front of **Star Tours**, the park's only simulator ride. Here you're ushered into a 'starspeeder' for a madcap journey through the cosmos. The

Kermit and Miss Piggy star in Muppet Vision 3-D!

ride isn't particularly frightening, but it does give passengers a good shake. Those who are prone to motion sickness may want to ask an attendant about seeing the movie in a stationary pod.

The atmosphere takes on an urban, brick-and-mortar quality as you drift into the area around New York Street. Here you'll find a statue of Miss Piggy standing in front of a theater showing **Jim Henson's Muppet Vision 3-D!**, a raucous 25-minute romp with Kermit, Piggy, and the rest of the muppet crew.

Nobody boils down a full-length movie into a 30-minute stage show quite like Disney, a fact amply proven yet again at the Backlot Theater, which features **The Hunchback of Notre Dame**. Elaborately costumed actors, some working puppets, belt out the animated film's most memorable tunes.

Exit the theater and wander over to **New York Street**, a backlot rendition of the Big Apple. Take a few moments to appreciate the extraordinary detail that went into its construction. The subtle street sounds – a distant siren, car horns, a jackhammer – are an especially nice touch.

Backstage Pass

It's a quick stroll down Commissary Lane and across the central plaza to **Mickey Avenue**. To the far left is the **Disney-MGM Studios Backlot Tour**, a 35-minute tram ride with glimpses of the wardrobe department, scenery workshop, and what appears to be a quiet suburban street lined with trim little houses. The buildings are only shells, of course, used in television commercials and programs. Later, the tram pulls into Catastrophe Canyon, which you're told is a movie set for a film currently under production. Within moments the earth begins to shake, an oil tanker explodes and a flash flood comes barreling toward you. The tour ends with an exhibit of show biz memorabilia at the **American Film Institute Showcase**.

Next up on Mickey Avenue is **Who Wants To Be a Millionaire – Play It!**, a re-creation of the game show, though contestants win Disney swag instead of cash. The audience plays along on individual keypads. Whoever gets the highest score becomes the next contestant.

At the end of Mickey Avenue in a little plaza called the **Animation Courtyard** is **The Magic of Disney Animation**, a tour of a working animation studio, including a presentation by an artist and a couple of interesting films, one featuring the unlikely team of actor Robin Williams and newsman Walter Cronkite. The last two shows – **The Voyage of the Little Mermaid** and **Playhouse Disney** – are sweet and schmaltzy, and best left to families with small children.

A Sporting Place

Sports fans should make a point of checking the schedule at Disney's Wide World of Sports, a $100-million, 200-acre (80-hectare) complex with a baseball stadium, a 5,000-seat basketball fieldhouse, 12 tennis courts and facilities for about 30 other sports. The complex is host to scores of amateur and professional competitions and is the home of Atlanta Braves spring training, Orlando Rays minor league baseball, and, in winter, the Harlem Globetrotters. The NFL Experience, a football program designed mostly for kids, is offered daily. The complex is on Victory Way near Disney-MGM Studios, just west of I-4. For a list of upcoming events, call (407) 939-1500; admission fees vary.

Disney's Animal Kingdom

Disney World's newest and largest theme park is essentially a state-of-the-art zoo dressed up in extravagant style. You realize you're in for something special the moment you walk through the front gates into an area known as **The Oasis** – a tropical garden laced with trails that lead past alcoves containing river otters, anteaters, sloths, and other small animals.

Emerging from The Oasis, you're greeted by a view of the **Tree of Life**, an artificial banyan-like tree that rises 14 stories above **Discovery Island**, set in a large lagoon connected by bridges to the park's four main 'lands.' What looks at first like the tree's gnarled bark are actually carved animal figures

Vulture perching in an enclosure

– more than 300 in all – that swirl around the trunk and limbs. Showing in a theater in the base of the tree is a 3-D movie, *It's Tough to be a Bug!*, based loosely on the Disney-Pixar movie *A Bug's Life*. The story involves seeing the world from an insect's point of view. You experience what it's like being on the receiving end of a fly swatter and encounter several noxious members of the insect family, including an acid-spraying termite and a stinkbug with, shall we say, a bad case of gas.

Walking around Discovery Island in a clockwise direction, the first bridge on the left leads to **Camp Minnie-Mickey**, designed in Adirondack style and devoted to live shows. The big attraction here is **Festival of the Lion King**, an uplifting 30-minute pageant based loosely on the animated film, with song, dance, acrobatics, and flamboyant costumes. The other show, **Pocahontas and Her Forest Friends**, is a morality tale intended for young children. Several pavilions used for character greetings

Lowland gorilla

are also best left to the little ones, unless you have a dire need to be photographed with Mickey.

Out of Africa, Into Asia

Return to Discovery Island and cross the first bridge on your left to **Africa**, where you immediately find yourself amid a clutch of stores and restaurants called **Harambe**, modeled loosely on a real-life Kenyan village. Next to an enormous, artificial baobab tree is the entrance to the park's most popular attraction, **Kilimanjaro Safaris**. Here visitors board safari vehicles for a 20-minute ride across a re-created patch of the African veldt. This being Disney, merely seeing lions, giraffes, zebras, and other wildlife isn't enough. About halfway through the tour, your driver learns that poachers are threatening an elephant mother and calf, and off you go on a wild ride to rescue the threatened beasts and catch the bad guys.

It's only a few steps from the safari exit to the **Pangani Forest Exploration Trail**, a nature walk where you can view endangered species like black-and-white colobus monkeys as well as hippos, gorillas, and meerkats. A research center harbors a colony of naked mole rats and a cleverly disguised aviary.

For an inside look at Disney World, sign up for one of the Behind-the-Scenes Tours. There are about 10 in all, including a backstage safari at Animal Kingdom, a tour of the underground 'utilidors' at the Magic Kingdom and a scuba diving adventure at EPCOT's Living Seas. For reservations, call (407) 939-8687.

If you're looking for a break from the crowds, you might consider a side trip to **Rafiki's Planet Watch**, a 'behind-the-scenes' area for environmental education. The journey starts with a ride on the **Wildlife Express**, a replica of a vintage steam locomotive that passes through the not-terribly-scenic 'backstage' area. At the end of the line is the **Conservation Station**, a veterinary facility with exhibits on animal care and protection.

Next door to Africa is **Asia,** a pastiche of thatched huts, stone spires and palace walls inspired by the traditional architecture of Thailand, Nepal, and India. Asia encompasses three main attractions. To your left as you enter is the Caravan Stage, presenting **Flights of Wonder**, a 20-minute show featuring hawks, falcons, parrots, and more than a dozen other birds. Also here is **Kali River Rapids**, a whitewater ride with a jungle setting and an environmental message. The final stop in Asia is the **Maharajah Jungle Trek**, a nature walk with views of Bengal tigers, fruit bats, and exotic birds.

Age of Dinosaurs

Return again to Discovery Island and cross the first bridge on the left to **DinoLand, USA**. You'll notice a more campy, carnival-like atmosphere here, injecting a welcome dose of humor into the mostly straight-faced approach elsewhere in the park. Walk past an elaborate kid's play area called The Boneyard and follow signs to **Dinosaur**, DinoLand's biggest thrill ride. The concept here is that you're transported back to the Age of Dinosaurs for a jolting ride through a misty Jurassic forest complete with falling meteors and hungry predators.

Next on the agenda is **Chester & Hester's Dino-Rama**, a mini-carnival intended primarily for children, with midway games and a couple of amusement-park rides. A large store, **Chester & Hester's Dinosaur Treasures**, is packed to the rafters with dino-related toys and novelties – a good place to pick up gifts for the kids back home.

The last big attraction in DinoLand is **Tarzan Rocks**, a live show that combines the energy of a rock concert and the high-flying acrobatics of the X Games. This is Disney World at its over-the-top best and a fitting way to end your day with a bang.

Downtown Disney

Downtown Disney is an entertainment complex on Lake Buena Vista about a mile (1.6km) east of Epcot. It's divided into three sections – West Side, Pleasure Island, and Marketplace – and is intended mostly for an adult audience.

The **West Side** is the least defined of the three areas, a mixed bag of restaurants, stores, and showplaces anchored on one end by **Cirque du Soleil**, a wildly imaginative theater troupe combining circus art and stagecraft, and on the other by **Planet Hollywood**, the well-known theme restaurant. In between are a few more restaurants, including **Wolfgang Puck** and **House of Blues** *(see Listings)*. You'll also find a place called **DisneyQuest**, a sort of pinball arcade on steroids, with cutting-edge video games and virtual-reality

West Side, Downtown Disney

rides. Loud and crowded, it has limited appeal for the post-pubescent. Nearby is a **Virgin Megastore**, with acres of floor space and dozens of listening stations. Several more specialty stores – ranging from cigars to guitars – are located in a building next door, which also houses a 24-screen movie theater playing all the latest blockbusters.

Pleasure Principle

Sometimes called 'Disney for adults,' **Pleasure Island** is a self-contained nightclub district with an adults-only policy (and cover charge) after 7pm. If you plan to make a night of it, the best strategy is to arrive early – say 8 or 9pm – and stop first at the **Comedy Warehouse**, home of a talented improv troupe that does several shows a night. There are also brief, seemingly impromptu comedy shows at the **Adventurers Club**, which is modeled after an old-fashioned, English gentlemen's club and staffed by a zany cast of characters.

If dancing is your thing, you have five venues to choose from. The premier dance club is **Mannequins**, a multilevel, warehouse-like facility with a viscera-quaking sound system, dazzling lights, and multiple bars. Elsewhere, the BET **Soundstage Club** specializes in hip-hop and R&B; **8Traxx** plays tunes from the 70s and 80s; **Motion** spins top-40 and alternative rock; and the **Rock 'n' Roll Beach Club** showcases live bands banging out classic rock. For a more laid-back experience, the **Pleasure Island Jazz Company** has some of the best combos in town. The festivities hit a high point at midnight, with fireworks, confetti, and a light show accompanied by a rock band at the outdoor **West End Stage**.

Marketplace occupies the eastern portion of Downtown Disney and is devoted to shopping. In addition to the world's largest Disney store are retailers carrying home furnishings, sports gear and toys. Far more interesting, even for adults, is the LEGO **Imagination Center**, if only for the LEGO sculptures displayed around the store. For eats, there's the **Ghi-rardelli Soda Fountain & Chocolate Shop**, a giant **McDon-ald's**, and one of Disney's two **Rainforest Cafes**, ensconced in what appears to be a smoldering volcano.

Disney's BoardWalk

You'll find a second and smaller entertainment complex at the BoardWalk, a fine spot for dining, dancing, and a romantic lakeside stroll.

Diners have a couple of good choices here. The **Flying Fish Cafe**, serving seafood, and **Spoodles**, specializing in Mediterranean cuisine, are both highly regarded, though sports fans may prefer the ESPN **Club**, a sports bar outfitted with more than 70 TV screens. Drinkers can sample hand-crafted suds at the **Big River Grille & Brewing Works** or join the singalong crowd at **Jellyrolls**, which features a rau-

R&B musician Sonny Rhodes at the House of Blues

cous dueling pianos act. Dancers can boogie at the **Atlantic Dancehall**, modeled after the classic dancehalls of the 1930s and 40s. DJs and live bands lay down the groove; wall-flowers can take advantage of the dance lessons that are offered most nights.

Disney's Water Parks

Water parks aren't for everybody, but if you're reasonably spry, don't mind hordes of rambunctious teens, and aren't self-conscious about walking around half naked, you'll have a blast flying down the various chutes and flumes or bobbing peacefully on one of the gentle 'river trips.'

A better fit for young adults is **Typhoon Lagoon**. Here you'll find a selection of high-speed slides as well as an enormous surf pool, a snorkeling trail where you can fin through the water with tropical fish and harmless sharks, and a relaxing 45-minute raft trip through rainforest grottoes and waterfalls. Mount Mayday, rising 90ft (27m) above the lagoon, has the wreck of a shrimp boat, the *Miss Tilly*, perched convincingly on its peak as if cast there by a passing tidal wave.

Blizzard Beach is Disney's newest water world and takes a different approach to the water park theme – one that is

---

Disney Cruises

Launched in 1998, the Disney Cruise Line sails two ships modeled after the luxury liners of the 1920s. Weeklong land-and-sea packages include 3 or 4 days at a Disney resort and the remainder at sea. Ships sail from Port Canaveral, an hour east of Orlando, to Nassau, Freeport and Castaway Cay in the Bahamas. This last destination, a tiny island, was a notorious hideout for drug smugglers until Disney transformed it into a private getaway. For information, call (800) 951-6499, or contact your travel agent.

decidedly chillier. This 66-acre (26-hectare) 'ski resort' surrounds Mount Gushmore, which swimmers may mount via chair lift. Attractions include Summit Plummet, which zips riders down a 350-ft (107m) ramp at speeds of 60mph (97kph) There are at least a dozen other slides, as well as the world's longest whitewater raft ride in which five passengers bob and twist through 1,200ft (360m) of standing waves, banked curves, and cataracts.

Hardrock Cafe, Universal Orlando

UNIVERSAL ORLANDO

Disney World's chief competitor is Universal Orlando, a complex of two theme parks, three hotels, and an entertainment district about 9 miles (15km) down I-4. Hipper than Mickey, with a knowing pop sensibility, Universal is especially appealing to teenagers and young adults who like big roller coasters, loud music, and action movies. That's not to say that Universal has forgotten everybody under 10 or over 50. Hardly. Kids get to pal around with the Rugrats, Barney, E.T. and other popular characters, while the gray-haired crowd enjoys tributes to Lucille Ball and Alfred Hitchcock, not to mention a selection of plush hotels and fine restaurants.

Universal Studios

Universal's flagship property is Universal Studios, a theme park inspired by the art and science of Hollywood movies. Sprawling across more than 400 acres (160 hectares), the park is laid out in a by-now familiar pattern: six themed 'neighborhoods,' each with its own rides and shows, arranged around a central lagoon. As Universal likes to remind us, this is a working production facility. Sections of the park double as movie sets, and several soundstages run by Nickelodeon Studios are used to tape children's television programs.

Welcome to Hollywood

The strains of 'Hooray for Hollywood' greet visitors as they pass through the front gate and file down **Plaza of the Stars**, surrounded on either side by souvenir stores and tourists snapping photos with costumed characters like Woody Woodpecker and Bullwinkle. If you veer right onto Rodeo Drive, you can peek into **Lucy: A Tribute**, an exhibit on the career of Lucille Ball, with video clips, memorabilia, and the obligatory gift store. There's nothing particularly socko about the exhibit, but those who grew up with Lucy and Ricky will be instantly charmed.

Rodeo Drive winds through a version of **Hollywood** plucked from America's collective subconscious – Ciro's, the Beverly Wilshire Hotel, the Max Factor Studio, the Brown Derby. Heightening the festive mood are live shows that seem to erupt spontaneously on the sidewalk, most featuring celebrity look-alikes such as Carmen Miranda, Groucho Marks, and Marilyn Monroe. This is also where you'll find the first of the park's high-tech, high-adrenaline attractions, **Terminator 2: 3-D Battle Across Time**, starring original cast members Arnold Schwarzenegger and Linda Hamilton. The action

Hollywood Boulevard

is nonstop, the volume is ear-splitting and the 3-D effects – as well as the live-action sequences – are dazzling. Even fans of action movies may be shell-shocked by the experience.

Monster makeup demonstration

About a half block farther along is the **Gory, Gruesome & Grotesque Horror Make-Up Show**, the funniest attraction at the park. The show features a wisecracking special-effects expert and a straightman, who freely mix shtick with a short course on the finer points of stage blood, rubber knives, explosive squibs and other staples of the horror genre. It's a good-natured 25 minutes filled with inside jokes, deft improvising, and – a rarity at theme parks – a dose of off-color humor. After the show, you can stop for a burger across the street at **Mel's Drive-In** (from George Lucas's 1973 *American Graffiti*) and listen to a doowap group perform outside.

Fun with Nausea

Continue along the right side of the lagoon past **Woody Woodpecker's Kidzone**, an area devoted to youngsters. About the only thing of interest to adults here is **Animal Planet Live!**, a show demonstrating how animal trainers and their charges work together behind the scenes.

Just beyond Animal Planet is a section of the park called

State-of-the-art simulator ride

World Expo, with two of the park's biggest attractions. If thrill rides are your thing, you're going to love **Back to the Future ... The Ride**, a head-spinning journey through time that sends you skittering over Ice Age glaciers, through a volcano, into the gullet of a dinosaur and, well, back to the future. Your conveyance is an eight-person motion simulator (it looks like the DeLorean from the movie) that moves in sync with images projected on a seven-story screen. What follows is five minutes of nonstop (some might say harrowing) action.

Lines are also usually quite long at **Men in Black: Alien Attack**, which Universal bills as a 'ride-through video game.' What you have here is a combination of a traditional dark ride and a shooting gallery. Each rider is equipped with a laser gun and instructed to shoot as many aliens as possible. The more aliens you zap, the higher your score. The only hitch is that the aliens shoot back, sending your vehicle into a wild tailspin with every hit.

Shark Attack

Continue counter-clockwise around the lagoon toward the cobblestone streets of **Amity**, the cinematic home of Sheriff Brody, Captain Quint, and a certain ill-tempered shark. Tourists can't resist posing for photos with a fiberglass shark hung from a scaffold in the main plaza, usually with their heads in its gaping maw.

Tucked behind a bank of trees a short walk from the plaza is a covered theater featuring the **Wild Wild Wild West Stunt**

Show, a 20-minute, bare-knuckle romp replete with gunfire, explosions, fistfights, and slapstick humor. Bottles are smashed over skulls, chairs are broken over backs, a guy falls off a roof, and the bank goes boom. It's goofy, good-natured, and generally benign and, being Universal, full of pyrotechnics.

Also just a few steps from the plaza is **Jaws**, Amity's signature attraction, in which a pleasant boat ride is rudely interrupted by you know who. It's that pesky shark, who shakes things up considerably despite the grenade launcher your 'guide' fires at him. There are bumps, surprises, screams, and the requisite number of explosions before you are returned to the safety of the dock, somewhat soggier but none the worse for wear.

A little farther along, Amity melds into **San Francisco**, home of **Earthquake – The Big One**, a three-part attraction inspired by the 1974 disaster film of the same name. In the first two parts of the show you watch a film about special effects narrated by Charlton Heston, then several volunteers re-enact a scene from the movie in order to demonstrate the use of blue-screen technology, a process in which images of actors are married with a background that's dropped in digitally. The finale starts when you board a 'subway train' for a simulated ride to Embarcadero

Posing with Jaws in Amityville

> **Universal knows how to party. Mardi Gras, Independence Day, Halloween and Christmas are celebrated with concerts, parades, fireworks, and other festivities. The celebrations last anywhere from a couple of days to a few weeks.**

Station. In the wink of an eye, you're in the midst of a catastrophic temblor that registers 8.3 on the Richter scale. The train shakes, the platform buckles, the ceiling collapses. A propane tanker comes crashing in from above and is engulfed in flame. Then water starts pouring in, thousands of gallons gushing through every crack and crevice in only a few seconds. And just when you think it's over, a runaway train comes hurtling straight at you. 'Cut!' a director yells, and the mayhem subsides just as quickly as it began. Pretty cool stuff.

It's a short walk down the Embarcadero and around the corner of Canal Street to **Beetlejuice's Rock 'n' Roll Graveyard Revue**, a goofy, raucous, almost painfully loud live show in which Beetlejuice (the wacky, stream-of-conscience ghoul from the Tim Burton flick), Frankenstein's monster, Dracula, Wolf Man, and the Bride of Frankenstein sing and dance to prerecorded tracks of rock classics. What the performance lacks in finesse it makes up for in energy and, no surprise, lots of pyrotechnics.

New York, New York

The movie-set metaphor becomes a reality in **New York**, which is a working back-lot. It's not unusual for a section of this area to be roped off while camera crews are at work. If you need a break from the crowds and rides, you might take some time to explore the back alleys and brownstones of 'downtown' or examine the scaled-down replicas of the Guggenheim Museum and New York Public Library.

Two shows are performed in the streets: the **Blues Brothers** feature Jake and Elwood look-alikes who do an enthusiastic 20 minutes of R&B standards on a tiny stage on Delancey Street. **Street Breaks**, a break-dancing troupe, performs at the intersection of 57th Street and Seventh Avenue.

On the corner you'll find **Twister… Ride It Out**, another three-part lesson in special effects similar to Earthquake. In this case, you first hear a spiel on tornadoes given by Helen Hunt and Bill Paxton, stars of the 1996 movie, then walk through a re-creation of a movie set. The payoff doesn't start until you file into a sound stage where the audience sees what appears to be an Oklahoma drive-in theater. What happens next is little short of amazing, as a five-story funnel cloud peels off roofs, rips out power lines and sends an assortment of objects – a billboard, a truck, a cow – flying through the air. It's all over in about two minutes, but they are two minutes worth waiting for.

A replica of Mel's Drive-In from the 1973 movie *American Graffiti*

Tickets for broadcast tapings at Nickelodeon Studios are available on a first-come, first-served basis. Call (407) 224-6355 for scheduling information or go directly to the Studio Audience Center to the right of the park entrance.

Lights, Camera, Action

The final section of the park is **Production Central**. Two new attractions are slated to open here in 2003. The first, housed in a castle-like building on Plaza of the Stars, is **Shrek 4-D**, a multisensory experience that picks up the story of the soft-hearted ogre where the 2001 animated movie left off. While waiting in the lobby, you learn that the ghost of Lord Farquaad (who was swallowed by a lovesick dragon in the first film) is plotting to exact revenge against Shrek and his new bride Princess Fiona by crashing their honeymoon with a host of ghoulish monsters. The action quickly evolves into an aerial dogfight involving fire-breathing dragons and a breathtaking plummet down a 300-ft (90m) waterfall. The 3-D images are enhanced by special effects built into the theater itself. Seats move up and down and side to side and are equipped with 'tactile transducers, pneumatic air propulsion, and water spray nodules.'

Just across the street is **The Neutron Adventure**, featuring yet another computer-generated character – Jimmy Neutron, Boy Genius. After watching a video setting up the action, guests file into a movie theater equipped with several rows of motion simulators in front of a huge screen. What follows is a madcap tour of Nickelodeon's cartoon universe in a spaceship piloted by the young Mr Neutron, who has to save the world from wicked egg-shaped aliens known as Yokians. The show is targeted squarely at kids, but adults will find it moderately entertaining.

Tucked behind The Neutron Adventure, fronted by a fountain that belches green, gooey 'slime,' is **Nickelodeon Studios**, the main production facility for the popular children's television network. The 30-minute studio tour is your best opportunity for a behind-the-scenes look at the making of real-life television shows. The tour is designed for kids but presents enough information to keep adults reasonably interested. Skip it if you're short on time.

Islands of Adventure

Just next door to Universal Studios is Islands of Adventure, Universal's newest park, featuring cutting-edge rides in five 'islands' arrayed around a central lagoon. The elaborate theming lavished on this park is evident the moment you pass through the gates and walk through the **Port of Entry**, a 'transitional zone' that's intended to evoke the exotic seaports of the East. There aren't any attractions here, but it's a good place to provision yourself with last-minute necessities – sunglasses, film, bottled water and such – all about 50 percent more expensive than in the 'real world.'

Port of Entry

The Doctor is In

If you bear right at the end of the Port of Entry, you come to **Seuss Landing**, inspired by the books of Theodor Seuss Geisel, aka Dr Seuss. Although it's designed for kids, adults too can't help but be tickled by this realization of Seuss's technicolor universe, where everything tilts, sags, and pitches to one side, with nary a right angle in sight. The rides are for kids, of course, but there's no reason grownups can't take a spin on the **Caro-Seuss-el**, a merry-go-round with Seussian creatures, or **The Cat in the Hat**, a dark ride that recounts one of the doctor's most beloved stories. You can even order a green-eggs-and-ham sandwich at an outdoor burger stand.

Gods and Monsters

The park takes a decidedly dark turn when you cross over a massive timber bridge into **The Lost Continent** – a dungeons-and-dragons fantasy come to life, about equal parts Middle Ages, Middle East, and Middle Earth. This is the site of **Mythos**, the park's finest restaurant, set within a 'mountain' whose craggy surface is carved with the face of some

Dueling Dragons, a double inverted coaster with intertwining tracks

long-forgotten deity, water gushing from his mouth.

Across the way, in what appears to be the ruins of an ancient temple, is **Poseidon's Fury**, a 21st-century update of a classic haunted house *(see picture on page 50)*. In this version, visitors are led through a series of chambers by an anxious guide who, in the tour's culminating sequence, is drafted into a battle between Poseidon and Zeus. What follows is about 5 minutes of finely orchestrated chaos replete with fireballs and watery explosions. The action is loud enough to wake the dead, but the effects – including a walk-through vortex involving more than 17,500 gallons (66,200 liters) of water – are quite dazzling.

A cast member from The Eighth Voyage of Sinbad

The same incendiary impulse is evident in **The Eighth Voyage of Sinbad**, a stunt show presented in a 1,200-seat amphitheater. Masterpiece Theatre it's not, though some adults may appreciate the deft stunt work, corny humor, and scorching pyrotechnics.

A litle farther along in the Lost Continent is the first of the park's monster roller coasters. Called **Dueling Dragons**, it's actually two separate coasters on intertwining tracks devilishly engineered for several near misses at speeds in excess of 55mph (89kph). This is an inverted coaster (the cars attach to the track overhead, while your legs dangle below), with multiple loops, corkscrews, and barrel rolls that subject riders to as much as 5Gs. Needless to say, only seasoned roller coaster aficionados should attempt this ride. Expect an extremely long line for all but the earliest and latest runs.

Poseidon's Fury

More Dinosaurs

The next 'island,' **Jurassic Park**, is the largest section of the park and will be immediately familiar to anyone who saw the 1993 Steven Spielberg movie. On the left after you pass through the imposing stone gateway is the **Jurassic Park Discovery Center**, a re-creation of the lodge from the movie, including a pair of dinosaur skeletons mounted in the atrium. Around the edges are a variety of interactive computer displays designed more for entertainment than education. In one exhibit you can 'meld' your DNA with that of a dinosaur, producing a composite of your face and a dinosaur's. Another allows you to analyze the contents of a dinosaur egg created in the Jurassic Park 'nursery.' The most fun is an exhibit called **You Bet Your Jurassic** that pits three live contestants against a wisecracking, computerized game-show host.

Farther along the main path is the **Triceratops Discovery Trail**, a low-key stroll through a 'veterinary compound' where visitors can watch animatronic dinos being weighed, measured, and fed. Even more amusing than the dinosaurs is watching young kids puzzle over the possibility that the beasts are real.

Across the way from the Discovery Trail is the island's big ride – the **Jurassic Park River Adventure**. Almost always crowded, the attraction takes you on what's billed as a peaceful float trip through dinosaur habitat. Things go awry almost immediately, and before you know it you're face to face with a hungry T-rex. The only way out is a stomach-flipping, 85-ft (26m) plummet. As the video monitors warn at the beginning of the ride: 'You will get wet and probably soaked.'

On the opposite side of the path is **Camp Jurassic**, an elaborate children's playground. Adults may want to wander around in order to appreciate the design; otherwise there's little reason to spend time here. The one ride in this section, **Pteranodon Flyers** (a modified ski lift that zooms overhead), is restricted to adults with children. A word of warning: kids love to ambush passersby with high-powered squirt guns stationed in the playground. Don't be surprised if you're the victim of a good-natured spritzing.

Toon Town

The atmosphere turns giddy the moment you cross over the bridge from Jurassic Park to **Toon Lagoon**, an entire 'island' devoted to cartoon characters like Blondie, Popeye, Betty Boop, and other familiar faces from the funny papers. The big attractions here are water rides. Expect to get drenched on **Popeye & Bluto's Bilge-Rat Barges**, a raft ride in which passengers are soaked with waterfalls, fountains, and spectators shooting water cannons. There are a few thrills and spills along the way but nothing too traumatic. Most of the fun comes from watching your shipmates getting doused, and wondering when your turn will come around.

Jurassic Park Discovery Center

Also here is a log flume ride called **Dudley Do-Right's Ripsaw Falls**. There's nothing new in the basic concept, although, like the Popeye ride, the set design is cleverly executed, employing the same off-the-wall humor as Dudley Do-Right's creator, animator Jay Ward. This one has more dips and drops than Bilge-Rat Barges, with a 75-ft (23m) plunge at the end that will make your stomach do a somersault and probably soak you to the skin.

Men in Tights

You enter a cartoon universe of a very different flavor at **Marvel Super Hero Island**, inspired by the comic book publisher who made superheroes out of flamboyantly attired fellows with bulging muscles. The overall design is more subdued than in Toon Lagoon, recalling the mean streets of New York with foreshortened skyscrapers and lots of faux chrome, steel, and glass.

The first attraction you come to is **The Amazing Adventures of Spider-Man**, hands down the best ride in the park and perhaps in all of Orlando. Spider-Man combines simulator technology and 3-D visuals in order to bring the comics to life. Along the way you

The Spider-Man ride

encounter a small army of evil-doers who send your tram into wild spins and lurches. The tour culminates in what feels like a headlong plunge into the city streets below, only to be saved at the last moment by – who else? – your friendly neighborhood Spider-Man. The amazing thing about this last maneuver is that your tram never moves more than 4ft (1.2m), although you'll have a hard time convincing your brain of that fact. Most adults will find the ride thrilling without being terrifying and, because it relies more on tricks of perception than physical jolts, it gives a good jostle without scrambling your innards.

The other big rides in this area should be reserved for the seasoned thrill seeker. **Dr Doom's Fearfall** is a common amusement-park ride that shoots passengers into the air and allows them to fall safely back to earth. In this version, riders are

Incredible Hulk Coaster

strapped into a four-person 'fear-sucking' chamber and rocketed 150ft (45m) straight up at a force of 4Gs, then pushed down faster than the speed of gravity. Just when you think you're safely back on earth, you do it all over again.

A bit farther along is the **Incredible Hulk Coaster**, another scream machine on a par with (and some would say even more dizzying than) Dueling Dragons. This one starts off with a bang, catapulting riders skyward with the G-force of an F-16 fighter. What follows in the next 2½ minutes is a short course in vertigo, as the cars scream through three rolls, two 'carousels,' two loops, and two subterranean passages, one of them *under* the lagoon. Top speed: a searing 67mph (108kph). Smile when you get to the end – they're taking your picture!

Much tamer, although nauseating in its own way, is **Storm Force Accelatron**, a Marvel-ized version of the 'teacups' – a spinning cup on a spinning disk on a spinning turntable. The effect, predictably, is dizzying.

CityWalk

Citywalk serves two purposes. During the day it functions as Universal's front porch. All visitors arriving by car must first pass through the CityWalk complex and its gauntlet of stores and restaurants before entering one of the theme parks. In the evening it becomes Universal's nightclub district, with dining, dancing, music, and a ready supply of liquor.

Most notable (and expensive) among the restaurants is **Emeril's** *(see Listings)*, created by celebrity chef Emeril Lagasse, who whips up beautifully prepared entrees laced with assertive Cajun flavors. The wine cellar is stocked with

CityWalk has the world's largest Hard Rock Cafe

12,000 bottles, and the waiting list is very, very long. Call for reservations well in advance. **Pastamoré**, a contemporary Italian just a few doors away, is also good – more casual, less expensive, and easier to get into on short notice.

Not surprisingly, theme restaurants are also well represented, and the grandaddy of 'em all is the **Hard Rock Cafe**. With seating for 600 in the restaurant and 3,000 in an adjoining concert hall, this is the largest Hard Rock in the world. Like its humbler brethren, the walls are plastered with gold records, instruments, and costumes, not to mention a pink Cadillac suspended over the bar and giant stained-glass panels depicting Elvis Presley, Chuck Berry, and Jerry Lee Lewis. American fare like burgers, steaks, and ribs – while not haute cuisine – is pretty good, and the servings are large enough to satisfy Elvis on an eating binge.

> **Emeril's (tel: 407-224-2424) is the only CityWalk restaurant that accepts reservations. A few others have 'priority seating,' which means your party has dibs on the first available table at or after your appointed time. Call (407) 224-9255 for details.**

Next to the Hard Rock is NBA **City**, a sports bar and restaurant dedicated to professional basketball, with skill games, player tributes, and dozens of TV screens. The lacquered, hardwood floors, and basketball hoops aren't merely decorations. When basketball stars drop by for a visit, the tables can be pushed aside for on-the-spot demonstrations.

Fans of stock-car racing should make a point of checking out the NASCAR **Cafe**, a shrine to the men (and women) and machines who make driving in circles one of America's top spectator sports. The menu features chicken wings, chili, burgers, and other rib-sticking dishes. Stock cars are displayed outside the restaurant and a couple actually hang from the ceiling inside.

Booze and Schmooze

For serious partyers, CityWalk doesn't heat up until about 10pm, by which time the nightclubs are in full swing and the crowd is properly lubricated. Expect to pay a cover charge at the door (times and fees vary) or, if you plan to go club-hopping, buy an all-in-one Party Pass for about $8 at the guest service kiosk near the entrance.

With seven themed nightclubs, CityWalk offers enough variety to satisfy just about any mood or taste in music. Most places serve food as well as drink and have live bands and plenty of room for dancing. At the **Motown Cafe**, for example, diners can sample sweet potato fritters, baby back ribs, and other Southern specialties, then shimmy the night away to the sweet strains of Motown sound-alikes singing classic songs by the Supremes, Temptations, and other hit makers.

Dancing at the groove

Reggae is king next door at **Bob Marley – A Tribute to Freedom**, modeled after Marley's Jamaica home. There's jerk chicken, fish chowder, and other Caribbean dishes on the menu, ice-cold Red Stripe beer at the bar, and either DJs or live bands laying down the beat.

A more mature crowd hangs out at **Pat O'Brien's**, a replica of a landmark New Orleans water hole. A raucous 'dueling pianos' act supplies music and laughs, while the kitchen turns out Creole creations such as jambalaya, po' boys, and gumbo. O'Brien's specialty in the libations department is the Hurricane, a rum concoction that packs a wallop.

Belly tops and body piercings are de rigueur at **the groove**, a cavernous dance club with hallucinogenic

Jimmy Buffet's Margaritaville

lights, an overworked mist machine and a viscera-quaking sound system that throbs with the sounds of techno, house and hip-hop. A warren of 'color' rooms – red, blue, green – each with its own theme, bar, and color-coded drinks, is the place to chat with a new acquaintance.

The cultures and cuisine of 21 Latin American nations are celebrated at the **Latin Quarter**, where dinner is usually followed by a floor show and dancing. Instructors are often on hand to initiate wallflowers. The atmosphere is more laid-back at **Jimmy Buffet's Margaritaville**, a reflection of the singer's beach bum persona. A margarita-spewing volcano keeps the crowd happy, and a house band rolls through Buffet's mellow songbook.

Around the bend is **CityJazz**, an intimate spot for some excellent jazz, with styles ranging from Chicago blues to bebop. The menu features light fare and about 60 wines. Or simply choose a drink from the rolling martini cart. More than 500 objects are on display here in *Downbeat* magazine's Jazz Hall of Fame.

As if all this weren't enough, there's also the **Universal Cineplex**, a modern movie palace with stadium seating and all the high-tech bells and whistles a moviegoer could ask for.

SEAWORLD

On I-4 between Disney World and Universal is SeaWorld, Orlando's third most popular theme park. With only two major rides, the atmosphere is quite different here: there are fewer lines and it's less frenetic. The pace suits the park's overall theme, because the wonder of this place doesn't come from thrill rides or shows – as good as they are – but from the fascinating array of marine animals and the opportunity to experience them up close. What turns people on is the rubbery feel of a dolphin's skin, the graceful flap of a stingrays 'wings,' and the sight of a 2-ton killer whale leaping into the air.

Water World

A cluster of attractions just beyond the entrance quickly puts visitors in an aquatic frame of mind. The **Tropical Reef** is an

Key West Dolphin Stadium

indoor exhibit with hundreds of brightly colored fish in illuminated aquariums; **Turtle Point** is a habitat for endangered turtle species, many of them nursed back to health after life-threatening injuries; and the **Dolphin Nursery** is a peaceful pool where dolphin mothers and calves spend time away from the bustle of theme-park life.

SeaWorld's entrance

Also in this area is the SeaWorld Theater, featuring **Pets Ahoy!**, a delightful show starring a four-legged cast of dogs, cats, pigs, a horse, even rats, who have been trained to do amazing tricks and comedy routines. Most of the animals were rescued from animal shelters.

The big show on this side of the park is at the **Key West Dolphin Stadium**, where a cast of bottlenose dolphins and false killer whales puts on a 20-minute display of waterborne acrobatics under the direction of their trainers, one of whom is catapulted into the air by these surprisingly powerful creatures.

You can touch the dolphins at **Dolphin Cove** just outside the stadium – that is, if you can convince them to come close enough. Your odds are a heck of a lot better during scheduled feeding times, when visitors can buy a paper cone filled with smelts. Like goats at a petting zoo, the dolphins come to the side of the pool to cadge their share of the feast. If the feeding area is too crowded – and it often is – stroll around to the underwater viewing bay for a different perspective on these highly social and intelligent animals.

The occupants of **Stingray Lagoon** aren't nearly as cuddly as their mammalian neighbors, but they're no less fascinating.

Here too guests are welcome to buy a tray of fish during scheduled meal times. Their stingers are intact but pose no threat as long as you're gentle.

Around the back of the stadium, in a 3½-acre (1.5-hectare) lagoon, is **Manatees: The Last Generation?**, home of a few of the 250 endangered Florida manatees rehabilitated by SeaWorld's Manatee Rescue Team. Also known as sea cows, these gentle, slow-moving mammals graze on aquatic vegetation in Florida's warm bays and estuaries, where they are prone to boat collisions. Some of the animals still bear scars or injured flippers. Those able to be rehabilitated are eventually returned to the wild.

Journey to Atlantis

Licensed to Thrill

There are only two thrill rides at SeaWorld, but both pack a wallop. The most benign is **Journey to Atlantis**, a cross between a log flume and a roller coaster. There's a story behind the ride involving the emergence of Atlantis, but with two 60-ft (18-m) plunges, several smaller dips, and a nonstop barrage of laser lights, you won't have a chance to follow along. Expect to get soaked, especially if you ride in the front seat.

Only hardcore thrill-seekers should consider riding **Kraken**, a monster roller coaster with a drop of 144ft (44m), seven inversions, three subterranean passages and a top speed of 65mph (105kph). Most diabolical of all is that this is a 'floorless' coaster, which means that your arms and legs dangle freely, with only a shoulder harness to stop you from sailing off into the stratosphere.

Penguins, Sea Lions, Sharks

Near the entrance to Kraken is **Penguin Encounter**, a chilly indoor habitat where a colony of the gregarious, flightless birds – denizens of Antarctica – huddle on the rocks and zip through the water with remarkable speed and agility. The air inside 30°F (-1°C), the water is 45°F (7°C), and 6,000 pounds (2,700kg) of snow fall every day.

The barking you hear in the distance isn't a pack of dogs but a colony of about 50 sea lions, who reside in a 2½-acre (1-hectare) habitat resembling the rugged coast of the Pacific Northwest, complete with crashing waves and rocky grottoes. Visitors can buy a tray of smelts to toss to the sea lions during feeding time.

Sea lions are the stars of the show next door at the **Sea Lion & Otter Stadium**, where they join a supporting cast of otters and walruses in a farce called **Clyde & Seamore Take Pirate**

Swimming with Sharks

If viewing sharks through acrylic isn't thrilling enough, consider getting into the water with them. SeaWorld's new Sharks Deep Dive program ($125–150) puts guests into a diving cage for a swim in the shark tank. Other 'animal interaction' experiences include a 2-hour training session with false killer whales ($200) and full-day programs in which you work side-by-side with a SeaWorld trainer or learn to rescue and rehabilitate manatees and other marine mammals ($389). Call (407) 351-3600 for information and reservations.

An underwater view of Shamu

Island. The story is goofy, and the actors have a tendency to 'improvise' unexpectedly, but the gaffes always get the biggest laughs. Try to arrive early. A mime warms up the crowd and does wicked impersonations of people filing into the stadium.

At the other side of the stadium is one of SeaWorld's newest attractions, **Terrors of the Deep**, devoted to some of the most dangerous creatures in the sea. The design of the exhibit is almost as fascinating as the animals themselves. Visitors file through a tunnel with clear acrylic walls while moray eels, barracudas, lion fish (whose venomous spines can be deadly to humans), and several kinds of sharks swim all around.

There's nothing particularly fishy about **Cirque de la Mer**, which plays at the Nautilus Theater next door to Terrors of the Deep. Nor is it a traditional circus. What you find instead is an imaginative combination of dance, acrobatics, comedy, and mime that draws on themes from – of all things – Incan mythology. Sounds weird but it works.

After the show, wander over to the **Clydesdale Hamlet** for a look at the statuesque draft horses who appear in Budweiser ads. If you're lucky, you'll see them being exercised by their keepers. SeaWorld is owned by Anheuser-Busch, brewers of Budweiser, Michelob, and other popular beers. Free samples are dispensed next door at the **Anheuser-Busch Hospitality Center**, which also offers a 30-minute **Beer School** for those who want to learn more about their favorite beverage or are considering brewing their own.

A Killer Named Shamu

Continue clockwise around the park to Shamu Stadium. Two shows are presented here, both starring Shamu, Baby Shamu, and Namu, a trio of killer whales, or orcas, who are put through their paces by a team of wetsuit-clad trainers. Some of the trainers actually jump into the water, ride on the whales' backs, cling to their massive fins, and get launched off their snouts high into the air. Television naturalist Jack Hanna appears intermittently via video to explain how the 'tricks' are related to the whales' natural behavior. In another highlight, Shamu soaks everyone sitting in the lower section with a flick of her mighty flukes. The splash zone is clearly marked; wear a rain poncho or sit at a higher level unless you're prepared to get drenched.

Atlantis Bayside Stadium

The 35-minute **Shamu Adventure Show** usually runs twice a day. A shorter program, **Shamu Rocks America**, plays in the evening. For another look at the whales, stroll around to an underwater viewing area called **Shamu: Close Up!** at the back of the stadium.

The excitement continues at the **Intensity Games Water Ski Show**, a 25-minute stunt exhibition at the **Atlantis Bayside Stadium** overlooking the park's 17-acre (7-hectare) lagoon. Ski jumpers soar through the air, waveboarders do high-velocity acrobatics, and barefoot skiers skim across the water's surface at lightning speed. This stadium is also the best spot to view SeaWorld's big finale. It's called the **Red, Bright & Blue Spectacular** and features fireworks, laser lights, and film images projected on sheets of water gushing into the air. The Spectacular is presented nightly during the busy season, approximately 45 minutes before closing.

While you're in this end of the park, be sure to visit **Wild Arctic**, a combination simulator ride and polar exhibit that takes you on a virtual helicopter ride to the Arctic Circle, including an encounter with real polar bears, housed inside a frigid and cavernous habitat. Those prone to motion sickness can opt to explore the Arctic 'by land.' An automatic side-walk transports you through the same exhibits without the abrupt movements.

Dolphin encounter at Discovery Cove

Also in the area is an elaborate children's play area called **Shamu's Happy Harbor** – of little interest to adults but a must if you're traveling with young children. Swan boats can be

> **Look out for Shamu's Splash Attack, where you can pay to sling water bombs at a friend. Ten water-filled balloons cost $5.**

rented for a quick paddle around the lagoon, and for a few extra bucks, the **Sky Tower**, a revolving, glassed-in platform that ascends a 400-ft (120-m) column, offers spectacular views of the park and surrounding area.

Discovery Cove

Adjacent to SeaWorld is a new and very different sort of theme park. SeaWorld calls it **Discovery Cove**, and it's more akin to a tropical resort than an amusement park. For starters, admission is limited to only 1,000 people per day, and guests pay a flat fee that includes everything they'll need – food, towels, wetsuits, masks, snorkels, lockers, sun screen. The only exceptions are alcoholic drinks and snacks.

What you get for your money is the freedom to roam a beautifully landscaped 32-acre (13-hectare) property where you can snorkel around an artificial coral reef stocked with tropical fish and a sunken ship (while sharks cruise behind a transparent barrier), float down a tropical river with rocky lagoons, waterfalls, a lush rainforest, and an aviary aflutter with exotic birds, or simply lounge beneath a palm tree on a white sandy beach.

For most visitors, the highlight of Discovery Cove is an opportunity to swim with a dolphin. 'Swim' may not be entirely accurate. What you do is interact with the animal under the watchful eye of a skilled trainer, who teaches you hand signals that cue the dolphin to roll over, wave flippers, exchange kisses, and tow you along.

BEYOND THE THEME PARKS

Newcomers to Orlando are often surprised at the variety of tourist attractions beyond the gates of Disney World, Universal, and SeaWorld. Not only are there several smaller theme parks but excellent museums, wilderness preserves, and quirky old-time attractions.

International Drive

Running alongside I-4 for about 10 miles (16km) between Disney World and downtown Orlando is International Drive, a tourist strip lined with hotels, restaurants, shopping plazas,

WonderWorks at Pointe Orlando

and several 'roadside attractions.' Typical of this last category is **Ripley's Believe It or Not! Odditorium** (8201 International Drive, tel: 407-363-4418; open daily 9am–midnight), a takeoff on Robert Ripley's books of oddities, with exhibits on sideshow staples like two-headed calves and curiosities like a Rolls-Royce made of matchsticks.

At **WonderWorks** (9067 International Drive, tel: 407-351-8800; open daily 9am–midnight) the emphasis is on science-related games and exhibits. It's worth driving by just to see the extraordinary building, which looks like an upside-down temple.

Skull Kingdom (5933 American Way, tel: 407-354-1564; open Mon–Fri 6pm–11.30pm, Sat–Sun noon–11.30pm), an elaborate haunted house with creepy stage sets and a ghoulish cast of characters, has a similar teen vibe. Visit on a lark for a laugh or two; otherwise, keep on driving. Same goes for **Pirates Cove Miniature Golf**, which has

The Holyland Experience

two elaborate 18-hole courses, and **Fun Spot Action Park**, a go-cart speedway and amusement park.

Of interest to enthusiasts is the **Train and Trolley Museum** (8990 International Drive, tel: 407-363-9002; open Mon–Sat 10am–9pm, Sun 10am–8pm), which features one of the largest model-train set-ups in the world, while **Titanic – Ship of Dreams** (8445 International Drive, tel: 877-410-1912 or 407-248-1166; open 10am–9pm) has exhibits of artifacts, re-creations of the ship's interior, and a staff of costumed guides.

Nearby, in its own futuristic building, is the **Hard Rock Vault** (8437 International Drive, tel: 407-599-7625; open daily 9am–midnight), an exhibition of rock 'n' roll memorabilia from the Hard Rock Cafe, chronicling rock music through various periods such as the British Invasion, the Psychedelic Sixties, and the advent of Punk Rock. Among the items on display are Jim Morrison's leather pants, Elvis's rhinestone cape, Buddy Holly's horn-rimmed glasses, and B.B. King's guitar 'Lucille.'

Yet another water park is at the northern end of International Drive just across from (and owned by) Universal Orlando. **Wet 'n' Wild** (6200 International Drive, tel: 407-351-1800; open daily 10am–6pm, extended summer hours) has a reputation for some of the hairiest slides in Orlando; adult visitors may prefer floating on an inner tube down the Lazy River.

Under the heading 'Only in Orlando' comes the **Holy Land Experience** (tel: 407-367-2065; open daily 10am–7pm, extended hours seasonally), a 'Christ-centered' theme park just beyond International Drive at 4655 Vineland Road. The brainchild of Jewish-born Baptist minister Marvin Rosenthal, the park re-creates ancient Jerusalem with scaled-down replicas of Herod's Temple, the Wilderness Tabernacle, Calvary Garden Tomb, and Qumran Dead Sea Caves. Elaborate multimedia shows and outdoor dramas feature actors in period costume. A new, $12-million Scriptorium houses an impressive collection of Biblical antiquities.

Kissimmee

South of Orlando, a short drive from Disney World, is Kissimmee, a small town chock-full of chain motels, fast-food joints and second-string attractions, most clustered around US 192.

Before Disney there was **Gatorland** (14501 Orange Blossom Trail, tel: 407-855-5496; open daily 9am–dusk), an old-fashioned tourist attraction that managed to survive the devel-

Alligator wrestling at Gatorland

opment of modern theme parks by sticking with a simple formula: if one alligator is good, thousands are better. Visitors can view breeding pens and nurseries, stroll through a cypress swamp, see exotic wildlife, and sample down-home delicacies like smoked gator ribs and deep-fried gator nuggets. Two shows keep visitors entertained: the   Gator

The Mysterious Kingdom of the Orient, the big show at Splendid China

Jumparoo Show, in which alligators leap out of the water to snatch a chicken from a trainer's hand, and the Gator Wrestling Cracker-style Show, featuring a wrangler who man-handles a big reptile. A new Trainer for a Day program lets visitors work side-by-side with a professional handler.

You'll find more exotic creatures at **Jungleland** (4580 West Irlo Bronson Memorial Highway; tel: 407-396-1012; open daily 9am–6pm), a zoo with alligators, big cats, and primates. The Bushmasters Gator Show is comparable to Gatorland's wrestling demonstration, while the Cat Show features some of Jungleland's felines – a collection that includes Bengal tigers, cougars, leopards, caracals, lions, and bobcats.

Also in Kissimmee is **Splendid China** (3000 Splendid China Boulevard, tel: 407-3967-8800; open: 9.30am–7pm), a 76-acre (31-hectare) park with more than 50 scale models of famous Chinese structures and landscapes, including the Temple of Confucius, Beijing's Forbidden City, and, a somewhat

Flying Tigers Warbird Museum

controversial choice, Lhasa's Potala Palace, home of the Dalai Lama before the Chinese occupation of Tibet. The detail is extraordinary. The model of the Great Wall, for example, is half a mile (0.8km) long and constructed with 6.5 million miniature bricks. Shows include 'The Mysterious Kingdom of the Orient', an extravagant 90-minute pageant combining ballet, folk dance, acrobatics, and lavish costuming. A second, shorter show features jugglers, plate-spinners, trapeze artists, and other acrobats – among the finest to come out of China. Puppet shows, craft exhibitions, storytelling, and martial arts demonstrations are offered throughout the day.

Feeling hot and bothered? You can cool off at **Water Mania** (6073 West Irlo Bronson Memorial Highway, tel: 407-239-8448; open daily 10am–5pm), where you'll find the usual array of chutes, tubes, and slides as well as a wave machine for those who want to try surfing on a boogey board.

Better suited to adult tastes is the **Flying Tigers Warbird Air Museum** (231 North Hoagland Boulevard, tel: 407-933-1942; open daily 9am–6pm), a working restoration facility for military aircraft. If you're interested in aviation or military history, the 45-minute guided tour is a must. Although the number and type of aircraft change regularly, you might see World War II bombers, Soviet MiGs, and American Skyhawk fighters as well as vintage biplanes and other aircraft from the early 20th century.

Gardeners should consider stopping at **A World of Orchids** (2501 Old Lake Wilson Road, tel: 407-396-1881), a conservatory brimming with lush tropical plants, including thousands of orchids, some quite rare. Those who prefer nature in a, well, natural setting, should visit the Nature Conservancy's **Disney Wilderness** (2700 Scrub Jay Trail, tel: 407-935-0002; open daily 9am–5pm,), a 12,000-acre (5,000-hectare) preserve with 7 miles (11km) of trails through wetlands and pine flatwoods ecosystems. Guided walks and 'buggy' tours are available.

DOWNTOWN ORLANDO

Orlando's compact downtown area is a hub for business and the arts, with stores, galleries and restaurants as well as gracious public spaces like **Lake Eola Park**, a 20-acre (8-hectare) oasis with an amphitheater, flowerbeds, walking trails, and swan-shaped paddle boats. Sadly, Church Street Station, an entertainment complex in a beautifully restored 19th-century train depot, is all but defunct, and plans for a revival remain uncertain.

The view across Lake Eola

A few blocks away, in the stately 1927 Orange County Courthouse, is the **Orange County Regional History Center** (65 East Central Boulevard, tel: 407-836-8500; open Mon–Sat 10am–5pm, Sun noon–5pm). Here four floors of exhibits chronicle the history of central Florida, starting with the region's native inhabitants and running through the arrival of European settlers

Refreshment is at hand

and 'cracker' cattlemen, the development of the citrus industry, and the growth of tourism from the earliest 'tin can tourists' to the construction of Disney World. Changing exhibits focus on a variety of topics, ranging in recent years from the 'rogues and rascals' of Florida's pioneer period and life in Orlando during World War II to the area's rock 'n' roll history.

Ella Fitzgerald, Duke Ellington, and Count Basie are just a few of the luminaries who stayed at the Wells Built Hotel, erected in 1929 by William Monroe Wells, Orlando's first African-American physician, for black musicians playing his downtown casino. Opened as the **Wells Built Museum of African American History and Culture** (511 West South Street, tel: 407-245-7535; open Mon–Fri 9am–5pm) in 2001, it now houses exhibitions on the life of African Americans in the segregated South.

African-American culture is also the subject of the tiny **Zora Neale Hurston National Museum of Fine Arts** (227

East Kennedy Boulevard, tel: 407-647-3307; open daily 9am–4pm) in nearby Eatonville, the first black township in the United States, founded in 1887. Raised in Eatonville, Hurston later became a prominent figure in the Harlem Renaissance, authoring books such as *Their Eyes Were Watching God* and *Of Men and Mules*. The gallery feaures work by African-American artists; an annual festival is held in Hurston's honor.

Loch Haven Park

Just north of downtown in lovely Loch Haven Park is a cluster of cultural institutions. The **Orlando Science Center** (777 East Princeton Street, tel: 407-514-2000; open Tues–Thur 9am–5pm, Fri–Sat 9am–9pm, Sun noon–5pm) encompasses 10 halls filled with interactive exhibits that, among other things, lead visitors on a journey through the human body, back to the Age of Dinosaurs, and across the cosmos. An eight-story domed theater, said to be the largest in the world, shows big-screen films, and sky shows are presented in the planetarium. Amateur skywatchers can join staff members for a night of stargazing at the center's Crosby Observatory.

On the opposite side of the park is the **Orlando Museum of Art** (2416 North Mills Avenue, tel: 407-896-4231; open Tues–Sat 10am–5pm, Sun noon–5pm), whose permanent collection of ancient American and African art and works by American painters such as Maurice Prendergast, John Singer Sargent, and Georgia O'Keeffe is supplemented by traveling exhibitions. Special events are held on the first Thursday evening

Orlando Science Center

A painting by Earl Cunningham at the Mennello Museum

of every month, with live music, a sample of cuisine from local restaurants, and exhibits by area artists.

So-called 'outsider art' is the focus of the **Mennello Museum of American Folk Art** (900 East Princeton Street, tel: 407-246-4278; open Tues–Sat 11am–5pm, Sun noon–5pm), also in the park overlooking Lake Formosa. In addition to hosting a variety of traveling exhibitions, the museum shows works from its permanent collection, largely dedicated to the 'primitive' paintings of Earl Cunningham, a tinker, sailor, chicken farmer, and self-taught artist whose brightly colored canvases have been acquired by several major museums, including the Metropolitan Museum of Art and the Smithsonian Institution.

It's a short drive from Loch Haven Park to the **Harry P. Leu Gardens and Historic House** (920 North Forest Avenue, tel: 407-246-2620; open daily 9am–5pm), where paths meander through 49 acres (20 hectares) of specialty gardens, including one of the South's largest collections of roses and camellias, and areas devoted to palms, herbs, tropical plants, and wetlands. 20-minute tours of the historic Leu House are offered throughout the day.

Leu Gardens provides a lovely, leafy background for a summer concert series featuring the Orlando Philharmonic Orchestra.

WINTER PARK AND MAITLAND

To the north of Orlando is Winter Park, an upscale suburb with a gracious, old-money atmosphere. Park Avenue is the town's main drag and good place for shopping, strolling, and a bite to eat when the tourist trails lose their charm. At the southern end of Park Avenue, on the trim Mediterranean-style campus of Rollins College, is the **Cornell Museum of Fine Arts** (tel: 407-646-2526; open Tues–Fri 10am–5pm, Sat–Sun 1pm–5pm), the oldest and one of the most distinguished art museums in Florida. The collection encompasses a wide range of European and American work, ranging from

Charles Hosmer Morse Museum of American Art

Renaissance and baroque masters to American landscapists like Thomas Moran and Albert Bierstadt, as well as a fair number of late 20th-century works.

Also associated with Rollins College is the **Charles Hosmer Morse Museum of American Art** (tel: 407-645-5324; open Tues–Sat 9.30am–4pm, Sun 1pm–4pm), a few blocks away at 445 Park Avenue. Though the museum's holdings include paintings by such notable American artists as George Inness, John Singer Sargent, Maurice Prendergast, and Thomas Hart Benton, the big attraction is an unmatched collection of stained glass by Louis Comfort Tiffany. The highlight of the collection, in addition to scores of windows, mosaics, lamps, and vessels, is a reconstruction of the Tiffany Chapel, designed for the 1893 World Columbian Exposition in Chicago.

Sculpture is the focus of the **Albin Polasek Museum and Sculpture Garden** (tel: 407-647-6294; open Tues–Sat 10am–4pm, Sun 1pm–4pm), located on three manicured acres a short walk from Rollins College at 633 Osceola Avenue. The collection of 200 works is dominated by the figurative sculpture of Albin Polasek, the Czech-American artist who lived and worked here before his death in 1965. Works by Augustus Saint-Gaudens, Nathaniel Hawthorne, and other American sculptors are displayed in the gallery and studio.

Maitland Museums

The vision of a single artist is very much in evidence a few miles north at the **Maitland Art Center** (tel: 407-644-1364; open Thur–Sun noon–4pm) at 221 West Packwood Avenue in suburban Maitland. Founded as an art colony in the 1930s by visionary artist and architect André Smith, the museum complex takes in galleries and studios designed in an idiosyncratic Aztec style set on 6 acres (2.5 hectares) of gardens and courtyards. Still an active art center, MAC offers instruction, lectures, concerts, and exhibitions of work by regional artists and selections from the permanent collection.

Several hundred wounded eagles, hawks, ospreys, owls, and other raptors are rescued and rehabilitated by the Florida Audubon Society's **Birds of Prey Center** (tel: 407-644-0190; open Tues–Sun 10am–4pm) at 1101 Audubon Way on Lake Sybelia. Although recuperating birds are kept in an isolated facility to minimize human contact, visitors can view members of about 32 species who are too severely injured to be returned to the wild.

A more somber experience awaits visitors at the small **Holocaust Memorial Resource and Education Center of Central Florida** (tel: 407-628-0555; open Mon–Thur 9am–4pm, Fri 9am–1pm, Sun 1pm–4pm) at 851 North Maitland Avenue. One room chronicles the history of the Holocaust with multimedia displays. Another offers changing exhibits on aspects of the Nazi campaign to exterminate Jews, homosexuals, gypsies, and other minorities.

FARTHER AFIELD

Beyond the greater Orlando area are even more theme parks and attractions, some dating to the early days of Florida tourism. **Cypress Gardens** (2641 South Lake Summit Drive, tel: 863-324-2111; open daily 9.30am–5pm) may be Florida's first theme park. It was established in 1936 and still lures travelers with old-time Southern charm, personified by the cast of parasol-twirling belles who stroll the grounds in hoop skirts and crinoline. Set in Winter Haven, about 50 miles (80km) southwest of Orlando, the park features a top-notch water-skiing show, a menagerie of exotic animals, performers from the Moscow Circus, and an outdoor concert series. The real heart of the place, however, is a 16-acre (6.5-hectare) botanical garden with theme areas ranging from a Southern Plantation Garden, Biblical Garden, and banyan-shaded Oriental Garden

Cypress Gardens, complete with Southern belles

to a conservatory filled with free-flying butterflies. The *Southern Breeze*, an authentic paddle boat, cruises the waters of scenic Lake Eloise.

Silver Springs (5656 East Silver Springs Boulevard, tel: 352-326-2121; open daily 10am–5pm), north of Orlando near Ocala, has been luring travelers with its crystal clear waters since the 1850s. Today, in addition to glass-bottom boats, which were invented here in 1878, the park offers cruises and Jeep tours through a wildlife habitat stocked with zebras, giraffes, antelopes, and other wildlife, as well as a cruise down a cypress-lined waterway alive with native Florida species such as alligators, osprey, and deer. Other animals are kept in naturalistic enclosures, including brown, black, and spectacled bears, rare Florida panthers, and a 2,000-pound (900-kg) crocodile thought to be the largest of its kind in captivity.

Weeki Wachee Springs (US Highway 19 and SR 50, tel: 877-469-3354; call for hours) has much the same appeal, although the activities here involve water sports – scuba diving, snorkeling, canoeing and water slides – as well as a wilderness cruise in search of otters, manatees, and water birds. Attracting the most attention are the mermaids – pretty girls in fishtails – who perform in the world's only 'underwater artesian spring theatre'.

Bigger, slicker and more commercial is **Busch Gardens** (tel: 813-987-5082; open daily 9.30am–6pm, extended summer and holiday hours), an Anheuser-Busch wildlife park in Tampa Bay. Safari tours, a primate reserve, a 70-acre (30-hectare) savanna, a Jeep rally, an excellent trainer-for-a-day program, and some 2,700 animals in naturalized environments reward visitors interested in wildlife, while a host of amusement-park

> **Special events at Cypress Gardens include the Spring Flower Festival from mid-March to mid-May, the Poinsettia Festival during the holiday season, and a year-round concert series.**

Busch Gardens usually runs five daily Serengeti Safaris, a 30-minute savanna tour in a flatbed truck surrounded by giraffes, zebras, and other wildlife. The fee is $30. Call (813) 984-4073 for reservations.

rides, including three of the biggest, baddest roller coasters in Florida, appeal to inveterate thrill seekers.

On the Atlantic Coast is the **Kennedy Space Center** ◄ (NASA Parkway, tel: 321-452-2121; open daily 9am–dusk), NASA's Florida headquarters and America's gateway to the heavens. At the Visitor Complex, exhibits on the history and technology of space travel often have a hands-on component, and there are live stage shows as well as IMAX films. Tours of the facility include a look at launch pads, mission control, and a full-scale replica of the space shuttle; astronauts are usually on hand to chat with visitors. Due to the tragic loss of Space Shuttle Columbia in February 2003, all Space Shuttle launches have been put on hold, and viewing tickets will therefore not be available for the foreseeable future.

Hundreds of other space-related artifacts are exhibited at the **Astronaut Hall of Fame** (6225 Vectorspace Boulevard, Titusville, tel: 321-269-6100; open daily 9am–5pm) about 6 miles (10km) west of the Kennedy Space Center. You'll also find an Astronaut Adventure interactive area, with a variety of training devices such as a G-force centrifuge, space shuttle simulator, and moon walk simulator.

When Nature Calls

Adjacent to the space center is 57,000-acre (23,000-hectare) **Canaveral National Seashore** (308 Julia Street, Titusville, tel: 386-428-3384; open daily 6am–8pm), whose miles of barrier dunes and beaches are a haven for beachcombers and nature lovers. Two of the beaches, **Apollo** and **Playalinda**, at the northern and southern tips of the Seashore, have restrooms, boardwalks and, from May 30 to September 1, lifeguards. In between, the landscape has been left blessedly untouched.

For a wilderness experience closer to Orlando, you have a choice of several parks, including **Blue Spring** and **Wekiva Springs State Parks** and **Lower Wekiva River Preserve**, where outdoor enthusiasts can swim or snorkel in crystal-clear springs and canoe on the St John and Wekiva Rivers. Canoeists and campers may prefer **Ocala National Forest** (17147 East Highway 40, Silver Springs, tel: 352-625-7470), 360,000 acres (146,000 hectares) of scrub oak ecosystem laced with slow-moving rivers, 'wet prairies,' and hundreds of ponds and lakes.

Those who prefer a tamer experience will appreciate **Bok Tower Gardens** (1151 Tower Boulevard, tel: 863-676-1408; open daily 8am–5pm), south of Orlando in Lake Wales. Established in 1929 by *Ladies' Home Journal* editor Edward Bok and designed by noted landscape architect Frederick Law Olmsted, Jr, the gardens' European-style plantings sprawl over 200 acres (80 hectares) of 'Iron Mountain,' Florida's highest point at about 975ft (300m). At the center of the grounds is the famous Singing Tower, a 209-ft-high (64-m) Arts and Crafts-style bell tower, housing one of only a few carillons in the United States. Recitals are presented daily.

Kennedy Space suit

WHAT TO DO

SHOPPING

In Orlando, shopping isn't merely about buying stuff, it's about 'retail entertainment.' Extravagant malls and specialty shops abound here, but you'll also find factory outlets and huge flea markets. There are even a few places where you can get Disney souvenirs at a discount.

Shopping in the Theme Parks

The theme parks are packed to the gills with stores of every size and description. Toys, T-shirts, and trinkets – notoriously overpriced – are the stock-in-trade of most vendors, although a few shops in every park offer merchandise that's sufficiently out of the ordinary to merit a second look.

At the Magic Kingdom, for example, you might want to have your mouse ears embroidered or try on a few of the outlandish hats at **Chapeau** on Main Street. Epcot has interesting imported goods at World Showcase, including fine glassware at **Il Bel Cristallo** in Italy and leather goods at **Tangier Traders** in Morocco. At Disney-MGM Studios, you'll find all sorts of odd Hollywood memorabilia – a pair of black pumps worn by Michelle Pfeiffer, bangles and baubles that belonged to Cher – at **Sid Cahuenga's One-of-a-Kind**. And shoppers with a taste for the dark side of the 'happiest place on Earth' might want a look-see at the **Beverly Sunset**, a souvenir shop dedicated to Disney villains.

The selection is more varied at Downtown Disney, with several huge non-Disney retailers, including a **Virgin Megastore** (tel: 407-828-0222) and the LEGO Imagination Center (tel: 407-828-0065), where kids and adults can create their own LEGO masterpieces in an outdoor play area and have their pictures taken with amazing LEGO 'sculptures'.

There are quite a few small specialty shops, too, including the **Guitar Gallery** (tel: 407-827-0118), which stocks about 150 instruments for would-be guitar gods, and **Sosa Family Cigar Company** (tel: 407-827-0114), where a professional cigar roller works in the front window and more than 80 brands of cigars are kept in a walk-in humidor. This is also home to **World of Disney**, the largest Disney store on the planet, a good place for doing all your souvenir shopping in one marathon session.

At Universal Studios there's the **Bates Motel Gift Shop**, with novelty items related to Alfred Hitchcock's *Psycho* such as a shower curtain with the Bates Motel logo or a button that says 'I love my mom!' The stores at Islands of Adventure are closely tied to the theme of each 'island.' At Seuss Landing, for example, you'll find a selection of T-shirts, plush toys and backpacks stamped with images of The Cat in the Hat and other Seuss characters. It's heartening to see one shop, **All the Books You Can Read**, stocked with the complete catalog of Dr Seuss titles. Fans of Marvel comics will want to browse Marvel Super Hero Island for a selection of the latest comic books and everything from coffee mugs to underpants emblazoned with pictures of their favorite characters.

Downtown Disney

Malls and Outlets

Beyond the theme parks, shoppers tend to congregate around the area's malls and outlets. **Belz Factory Outlet Mall** (5401 West Oakridge Road, tel: 407-354-0126; open Mon–Sat 10am–9pm, Sun 10am–6pm) is actually two malls plus a couple of annexes encompassing 170 outlets. The big attraction, of course, is deep discounts on

Plush toys at Universal Studios

designer clothes by Anne Klein, London Fog, Christian Dior, Tommy Hilfiger, and many others, as well as just about every brand of jeans, sneakers, and housewares. Fed up with the exorbitant price of souvenirs at the theme parks? The **Character Warehouse** (tel: 407-345-5285) offers bargains on overstocked Disney merchandise, and the **Universal Studios Outlet** (tel: 407-354-0126) does the same for Universal products.

The bargains continue at the **Lake Buena Vista Factory Stores** (15591 State Road 535, tel: 407-238-9301; open Mon–Sat 10am–9pm, Sun 10am–6pm), a much smaller but quite attractive complex with 40 stores, including Gap, Nine West, Old Navy, Murano Glass, Sony, and a Disney outlet called Character Corner. Maintaining a slightly higher profile is the **Orlando Premium Outlets** (8200 Vineland Avenue, tel: 407-238-7787; open Mon–Sat 10am–10pm, Sun 10am–9pm), which bills itself with the oxymoron 'upscale outlet center.' The stores are a bit swankier: Barney's, Brooks Brothers, DKNY, Armani, Versace, Coach, and other high-toned retailers. Disney and Universal Studios have stores here, too.

Take a typical American shopping mall, make it three or four times larger, and you wind up with something resem-

FAO **Schwarz at Pointe Orlando**

bling the **Florida Mall** (8001 South Orange Blossom Trail, tel: 407-855-1827; open Mon–Sat 10am–9.30pm, Sun 11am–6pm). With more than 250 specialty shops and six major department stores, this is central Florida's largest shopping destination.

Other shopping complexes rely on architecture, atmosphere and special attractions to lure customers. The **Mercado** (8445 International Drive, tel: 407-345-9337; open daily 10am–10pm), for example, is modeled after a Mediterranean village, with cobblestone paths, tile fountains, and a piazza for live entertainment. In addition to about 25 stores are Titanic–Ship of Dreams *(see page 67)* and a forthcoming museum of rock 'n' roll memorabilia drawn from the collection of the Hard Rock Cafe as well as a food court and several restaurants.

Pointe Orlando (9101 International Drive, tel: 407-248-2838; open Sun–Thur 10am–10pm, Fri–Sat 10am–11pm) has a similar appeal, with upscale, open-air shopping, live entertainment, WonderWorks *(see page 66)*, several bars and restaurants, and a 21-screen cineplex with an IMAX theater. Stores include Abercrombie & Fitch, Armani Exchange, Express and the Florida flagship of toy-seller FAO Schwarz.

Old Town Kissimmee (5770 US 192, tel: 407-396-4888; open daily 10am–11pm) has a more down-home feeling. A garden-variety amusement park fronts a strip of about 75 stores dressed up in old-timey, turn-of-the-20th-century style. Kissimmee is also the place for flea markets. There are three in the area: **Main Gate Flea Market** (5407 US 192, tel: 407-390-1015; open daily 10am–10pm), **192 Flea Market** (4301

West Vine Street at US 192, tel: 407-396-4555; open daily 9am–6pm), and **Osceola Flea and Farmers Market** (2801 US 192, tel: 407-846-2811; open Fri–Sun 8am–5pm).

For those who prefer a downtown setting, **Park Avenue** in Winter Garden is a trim, upper-crust neighborhood perfect for an afternoon of browsing the boutiques, galleries, and gourmet shops or stopping for coffee and Danish at a sidewalk cafe. Don't overlook the little courtyards off the main strip.

NIGHTLIFE AND THE PERFORMING ARTS

Schmaltz and special effects are the rule at the theme parks, but in the real world there's quite a bit of serious work being done in the performing arts.

Serious, in this case, refers to just about any mode of sincere expression, whether it's high-brow material – Shakespeare, Mozart, that sort of thing – or popular forms like Broadway shows and guitar-bashing rock 'n' roll. For a listing of the latest events, check the Calendar section of the Friday *Orlando Sentinel* or the free *Orlando Weekly*.

Motown Cafe, CityWalk

Theater

The most remarkable show in town is presented by **Cirque du Soleil** (tel: 407-939-7600), a troupe of about 100 performers who blend traditional circus art with theater, mime, cabaret, and illusion. The show, *La Nouba*, is as difficult to describe as it is entertaining. It's safe to say you've never experienced anything like it. The experience doesn't come cheap – at about $72 for an adult, the price comparable to a Broadway show – but most people say it's worth every penny. Cirque du Soleil is situated in Downtown Disney. See it if you can.

More traditional fare is offered in downtown Orlando at the **Bob Carr Performing Arts Centre** (401 West Livingstone Street, tel: 407-849-2001), which presents a regular schedule of Broadway road shows and performances by the Orlando Philharmonic Orchestra, Orlando Opera, and Orlando Ballet.

Lovers of the Bard will be delighted with the **Orlando-UCF Shakespeare Festival**, a professional company headquartered at the newly renovated **John & Rita Lowndes Shakespeare Center** (812 East Rollins Street, tel: 407-447-1700) in Loch

Cirque du Soleil

Haven Park. Despite the group's name, the repertoire isn't limited to Shakespeare. Of the five plays offered in a recent season, two – *Tartuffe* and *The Island of Dr Moreau* – were unrelated to Shakespeare. There's also a series

> **Half-price theater tickets for same-day performances can be purchased at OTIX, located in the Official Orlando Visitors Center (8723 International Drive).**

of children's shows, readings, and workshops.

More daring is a crop of small, independent theaters that have sprung up around town in recent years. The **Mad Cow Theatre** (105 East Pine Street, tel: 407-297-8788) has been garnering positive reviews for its interpretations of plays by a wide range of authors, including Anton Chekhov, Tennessee Williams, Neil Simon, and others. The historic **Church Street Theatre** (128 West Church Street, tel: 407-254-4930) presents the work of the **Orlando Youth Theatre**, which performs shows for kids *by* kids, and the **Orlando Black Essential Theatre**, an African-American company that presents five shows a season. **Impacte Productions** (237 University Park Drive, Winter Park, tel: 407-672-4868) is the brainchild of recent UCF theater grads and playwright Tod Kimbro, author of such off-the-wall comedies as *The Zombie Doorman* and *Suckers*. Kimbro and his troupe are favorites at the **Orlando International Fringe Festival**, a 10-day theater blowout with hundreds of performances by groups from around the world. Call (407) 648-0077 for information.

If you're in the mood for something light, look no further than the **SAK Theatre Comedy Lab** (398 West Amelia Street, tel: 407-648-0001), a hilarious improv troupe whose two main shows, *Duel of Fools* and *Fool Jam*, are staged like game shows.

Dinner theater is also enormously popular in Orlando. For details, see Eating Out.

Music and Dance

On the classical side of the musical score are the **Orlando Philharmonic** (tel: 407-896-6700), **Orlando Opera** (tel: 407-426-1700), and **Orlando Ballet** (tel: 407-426-1739), all favoring a repertoire drawn from the Western canon, though the ballet often mixes in contemporary pieces choreographed by artistic director Fernando Bujones. For information, call the companies or the Bob Carr Performing Arts Centre (407) 849-2001. Also worth catching is the **Bach Festival Choir and Orchestra** (1000 Holt Avenue, Winter Park, tel: 407-646-2182), which performs at Knowles Memorial Chapel on the Rollins College campus and other venues around Winter Park.

Those who prefer pop music should check the schedule at the **TD Waterhouse Centre** (tel: 407-849-2020), an arena in the Orlando Centroplex that is host to big-ticket performers as well as to sporting events. The **Hard Rock Cafe** (tel: 407-351-7625) at Universal's Citywalk and the **House of Blues** (tel: 407-934-2583) at Downtown Disney have much smaller venues and feature a mixed slate of classic rockers, hot new stars, and emerging talent. The Hard Rock has a 3,000-seat concert hall adjacent to the restaurant. The House of Blues is a 'club-style venue,' which means most of the audience stands.

Movies

There's no lack of choice for movie-goers, as you might expect in a town whose two biggest tourist attractions – Disney and Universal – are offshoots of movie studios. The 20-screen **Universal Cineplex** at CityWalk and the 24-screen AMC megaplex at Downtown Disney show the latest releases in theaters that have stadium seating, digital sound systems, and floor-to-ceiling screens. It's a shame that neither complex devotes at least one theater to foreign and alternative films or revivals of the golden oldies that must be collecting dust in the studio vaults. You'll find more of the same at the

Muvico Pointe 21 (9101 International Drive, tel: 407-926-6850) in the Pointe Orlando shopping plaza. Also here is a theater showing IMAX 3-D films.

The only art house in the area is the **Enzian Theater** (1300 South Orlando Avenue; tel: 407-629-0054) in Maitland. In addition to indie films, the theater sponsors the Florida Film Festival in June and specialty series like the South Asian and Jewish film festivals throughout the year. The Enzian also sponsors a series of classic movies shown outdoors on the third Thursday of each month in Central Park (free).

The sound of New Orleans at Pat O'Brien's, CityWalk

Nightclubs

In addition to Pleasure Island and CityWalk *(see page 54)*, there's a lively nightclub scene in downtown Orlando and on International Drive. At **:08 (8 Seconds)** (100 West Livingston Street, tel: 407-839-4800), for example, you'll find live country music, line dancing, a dozen bars and, on Saturday night, real-live bull riding. **Howl at the Moon** (55 West Church Street, tel: 407-841-9118) is a raucous sing-along club, where a pair of piano players bang out rock classics. **Mulvaney's** (27 West Church Street, tel: 407-872-3296) is an Irish pub with an excellent selection of imported brews and live Irish folk music. **Cairo** (22 South Magnolia Avenue, tel: 407-422-3595) is a dance club with three floors of music – reggae on the roof, house in the big room, and disco on the second floor. **Icon** (20 East Central Boulevard, tel: 407-649-6496), another dance club, has big-name DJs and an ultra-hip, 'post-apocalyptic' design.

On International Drive, at Pointe Orlando, is **XS Orlando** (9101 International Drive, tel: 407-226-8922), a dance hall and restaurant with simulator rides and state-of-the-art video games. Pointe Orlando also has **Metropolis** and **The Matrix** (tel: 407-370-3700), so-called 'European-style' dance clubs.

If you've had enough of laser lights and mind-numbing music, try **JB's Sports Bar** (4880 South Kirkman Road, tel: 407-293-8881), a good spot to have a beer and watch a ball game, or **Cricketers Arms** (8445 International Drive, tel: 407-354-0686), an English pub with lots of imported beers, broadcasts of European sports, live bands, and a lively expat crowd.

Bob Marley – A Tribute to Freedom

THE SPORTING LIFE

Whether you're a couch jockey or a true athlete, Orlando has more than enough sports-related activities to keep you happy. Balmy year-round weather makes the area a natural choice for golfers, fishermen, tennis players, and other out-doorsy types, and a great variety of athletic events are supported by legions of sports-crazed fans.

Birdies and Bogeys

With 150 courses to choose from, you can build an entire vacation around golf in Orlando. Disney World has five championship courses and 15 golf pros. Two courses near Disney, ultramodern **Villas at Grand Cypress Resort**, with a 45-hole course designed by Jack Nicklaus, and **Bay Hill Club and Lodge**, with its famed Arnold Palmer Golf Academy, are top rated. Palmer also designed **Orange Lake Resort and Country Club** at the quiet end of International Drive, while Nick Faldo put his stamp on two courses at Marriott's **Grand Vista Resort**, also on I-Drive.

There are more than 10 excellent **public courses** in the Orlando area, and the green fees are usually far less than those at the fancy private courses. For a complete list of courses, order a copy of the *Golfer's Guide* by calling (800) 864-6101 or have a look at <www.orlandogolfer.com>.

Tennis

Disney World resorts contain 25 tennis courts. Disney's **Racquet Club** at the Contemporary Resort is the highlight, with six clay courts and a professional shop. Call for reservations at (407) 939-7529. You can also make reservations for the courts at the Yacht and Beach Club by calling the number above. Courts at the Grand Floridian, Fort Wilderness, BoardWalk, Old Key West, and the Swan and Dolphin

The Orlando Magic plays at the TD Waterhouse Centre

are on a first-come, first-served basis. Courts are open from 7am to 7pm with the exception of the Swan and Dolphin, where they are open 24 hours. Play is often limited to two hours and there are fees at the Contemporary, Grand Floridian, and Swan and Dolphin. Disney also offers a rotating program of training sessions. Call the number above for details.

Outside Disney World, you can get information about court availability, lessons, and equipment rental from the **Orlando Tennis Service** at <www.orlandotennis.com> or by calling (888) 958-0487.

Gone Fishin'

The fishing is quite good at Disney World, and you don't need a state license. Bay Lake, Seven Seas Lagoon, and Crescent Lake are stocked with bass, and guided fishing excursions depart several times a day. Fees range from $180 to $210 for the first two hours, $80 for each additional hour. Reservations are required. For more information, call (407) 939-7529.

A state fishing license is required outside Disney. A 7-day license costs about $17 and is available at most sporting goods stores, Wal-Marts, and fishing camps. Check <www.floridaconservation.org/fishing> for information on fishing sites, conditions, and bag limits, or call (850) 488-1960 for the *Florida Fishing Handbook*, available from the Florida Game and Fresh Water Fish Commission.

Spectator Sports

The **Orlando Magic** (<www.nba.com/magic>) is the toughest ticket in town. The National Basketball Association hoopsters play in the 16,000-seat TD Waterhouse Centre (tel: 407-849-2020), formerly called the Orlando Arena. Tickets run from $10 to $90 and are virtually impossible to buy unless you reserve months in advance.

There's no National Football League team in Orlando, but there is arena football, a scaled-down version of the game played indoors with only eight men on a team. The **Orlando Predators** (<www.orlandopredators.net>) play at the TD Waterhouse Centre; tickets are $7.50 to $40.

Spring training

More than a dozen major league teams have spring training camps in Florida. Here are several close to Orlando.

Boston Red Sox: City of Palms Park, Fort Myers, tel: (941) 334-4700.
Chicago White Sox: Ed Smith Stadium, Sarasota, tel: (941) 954-7699.
Cincinnati Reds: Plant City Stadium, Plant City, tel: (813) 752-7337.
Detroit Tigers: Marchant Stadium, Lakeland, tel: (941) 603-6278.
Florida Marlins: Cocoa Expo, Cocoa, tel: (407) 639-9200.
Houston Astros: Osceola Stadium, Kissimmee, tel: (407) 933-2520.
Minnesota Twins: Lee County Sports Complex, Fort Myers, tel: (800) 338-9467.
Montreal Expos: Roger Dean Stadium, Jupiter, tel: (561) 775-1818.
New York Yankees: Legends Field, Tampa, tel: (813) 879-2244.
Philadelphia Phillies: Jack Russell Stadium, Clearwater, tel: (727) 442-8496.
Pittsburgh Pirates: McKechnie Field, Bradenton, tel: (941) 748-4610.
Tampa Bay Devil Rays: Lang Field, St Petersburg, tel: (727) 894-4773.
Texas Rangers: Charlotte Stadium, Port Charlotte, tel: (941) 625-9500.
Toronto Blue Jays: Dunedin Stadium, Dunedin, tel: (727) 733-0429.

Baseball fans can cheer for the Class AA **Orlando Rays** (<www.orlandorays.com>) at Disney's Wide World of Sports. Tickets are $5 to $10. The Disney complex is home to the **Atlanta Braves** spring training camp, too, as well as a wide range of professional and amateur competitions. Check <www.disneysports.com> for a schedule of upcoming events.

Disney is also home to the **Indy 200**, held in January at the Walt Disney World Speedway (tel: 407-939-7810).

Gamblers can bet on live jai-alai and horse racing simulcasts at **Orlando-Seminole Jai-Alai** (6405 US 17-92, Casselberry, tel: 407-339-6221), north of Orlando. There's also betting at **Seminole Greyhound Park** (200 Seminola Boulevard, Casselberry, tel: 407-699-4510).

Calendar of Events

January Disney World Marathon (first week in Jan).

February Mardi Gras celebrations at Pleasure Island and Universal Studios (mid-Feb through early April).

April Epcot's International Flower and Garden Festival (late April through early July).

May Star War Weekends at Disney-MGM Studios, featuring memorabilia trading, character greetings, and special presentations.

July Independence Day, fireworks at Disney World, Universal Studios, and Lake Eola in downtown Orlando (July 4).

September ABC Super Soap Weekend at Disney-MGM Studios, a soap opera convention (early Sept). Official Disneyana Convention, a week of trading, seminars and auctions at Epcot (first week in Sept).

October International Food and Wine Festival, Epcot (late Oct to late Nov). Halloween at Universal Studios and Disney World, with parades, costumes and special performances (mid to late Oct).

December Disney Magical Holidays features parades, concerts, and light shows, including snowfall on Main Street (late Dec to early Jan).

EATING OUT

When it comes to eating out in Orlando, there's good news and there's bad news. The goods news is that the restaurant scene has perked up in recent years, thanks largely to a crop of hot young chefs who are staking a claim to North America's top tourist market. The bad news – and this pertains mostly to the theme parks, especially Disney – is that the food is overpriced and often of poor quality.

THE BEST OF THE PARKS

There are a few exceptions. The **Hollywood Brown Derby** at Disney-MGM Studios is a cut above the competition, as are **Les Chefs de France** (and its less expensive upstairs counterpart Bistro de Paris), **San Angel Inn**, and **Restaurant Marrakesh** at Epcot's World Showcase. All are quite pricey, however, and the quality diminishes appreciably as you drop down to moderately priced eateries. Fast food, the cheapest option, is hardly a bargain; expect to spend $5–$6 for a burger and fries, about $2 for a soft drink.

The picture is brighter at Universal. Of particular note is **Mythos**, the high-end restaurant at Islands of Adventure. **Confisco Grill** is good for grazing on a variety of ethnic bites; the **Enchanted Oak Tavern** lets you gnaw on turkey legs and quaff beer in a building that looks like a gnarled tree stump; and **Croissant Moon Bakery** is a good spot to tank up on coffee, pastries, and sandwiches.

Within the parks, you'll do better at the entertainment complexes – Downtown Disney, Disney's BoardWalk, and Universal's CityWalk. **Wolfgang Puck** is the big draw at Downtown Disney. Pass on the formal dining room in favor of the downstairs cafe. It's livelier, more casual, and less expensive, and the food is just as good. You can't miss with

**Movie memorabilia fills Planet
Hollywood at Downtown Disney**

Puck's gourmet pizza, and the sushi bar is primo. The Southern-fried vittles at **House of Blues** are surprisingly good for a chain operation of this size. Gumbo, jambalaya, and Louisiana crawfish have an authentic tang, and the lineup of musical acts – especially at the Gospel Brunch – are a worthy complement to any meal.

The Creole fare is more inventive at **Emeril's**, the culinary standard-bearer at Universal's CityWalk created by celebrity chef Emeril Lagasse. The prices are sky-high and the waiting list can stretch for weeks, but if you're a real foodie it's worth the investment. **Pat O'Brien's** is a worthy runner-up. A replica of a New Orleans landmark, it serves po' boys, catfish, jambalaya, and other Louisiana specialties in iron skillets with wax-paper wrapping and plastic utensils. Wash your meal down with a Hurricane, a rum drink guaranteed to put you in a 'Big Easy' frame of mind.

Disney and Universal have also put a good deal of effort into elevating the quality of their hotel restaurants. Leading the pack is the **California Grill**, a picture of cool, contemporary elegance on the 15th floor of the Contemporary Hotel. If you enjoy watching chefs at work, request a seat at the counter. Otherwise, ask to be seated near a window in order to watch the fireworks over the Magic Kingdom. If the California Grill is Disney in a rare moment of tasteful restraint, then **Victoria & Albert's** at the Grand Floridian is just the opposite – a Victorian fantasy run amok. Florid, flouncy, and extremely expensive, it's the ultimate Disney experience for those who appreciate dining as theater. The seven-course gourmet feast is served by a white-gloved maid and butler named – what else? – Victoria and Albert. If money is no object, book the Chef's Table, where a chef will prepare dinner before your eyes. **Citricos** and **Narcoossee's**, also at the Grand Floridian, are fine choices, too.

The culinary flagship of Universal's three hotels is the **Delfino Riviera** at the Portofino Bay Hotel, a gorgeous setting for Ligurian cuisine. Less expensive but appealing in a low-key way is **Momma Della's Ristorante**, with homey standards like chicken cacciatore, veal scallopini, chicken parmigiana, and lasagna.

Themed Restaurants

Whatever the park restaurants lack in gastronomic finesse they more than compensate for in atmosphere. Indeed, Orlando's most lasting contribution to culinary history may be the development of the theme restaurant. Themes vary widely and

---

Dine with Character

Character dining – that is, eating at a restaurant where Mickey and other costumed characters make an appearance – is a quintessential Disney experience and surprisingly fun even for grownups. Among the best options for adults are the breakfast buffet at Chef Mickey's (Contemporary Hotel), the breakfast or lunch buffet at the Crystal Palace (Magic Kingdom), the breakfast buffet at the Cape May Cafe (Beach Club resort), and breakfast at Artist Point (Wilderness Lodge).

At Disney, reservations are known as 'priority seating.' Essentially, your party has dibs on the first available table at or after your appointed time. As always, restaurants are least crowded during off-hours. Plan on a late lunch or early dinner.

may have little, if anything, to do with food. In most cases, in fact, food is entirely beside the point. The two best-known theme restaurants, the **Hard Rock Cafe** (at Universal's CityWalk) and **Planet Hollywood** (at Downtown Disney), have spawned a brood of smaller operations catering to special interests of every sort.

At Universal, for example, there's NBA **City** (dedicated to pro basketball), the **Motown Cafe, Bob Marley – A Tribute to Freedom**, a place in Seuss Landing where you can order a green egg and ham sandwich, and the NASCAR **Cafe**, which is only one of two theme restaurants in Orlando devoted to motor sports. The other, **Race Rock**, is on International Drive. Over at Disney, theme restaurants range from the **Sci-Fi Dine-in Theater**, a re-creation of a 1950s drive-in movie at Disney-MGM Studios, where customers sit in vintage 'convertibles' and watch hokey sci-fi trailers, to the jungle-like ambience of the **Rainforest Cafe** which, by the way, doesn't actually have any rainforest-related foods on the menu.

OUTSIDE THE PARKS

Restaurants outside the parks are more varied and less expensive, though you'll have to sift through a sea of fast-food joints to get to the good ones. Sophisticated, contemporary dining is the forte of smart downtown eateries like **Manuel's on the 28th** and the **Boheme** at the Westin Grand Bohemian Hotel.

For sheer value, however, you can't beat small, family-run ethnic restaurants. They keep a low profile but inject a welcome strain of authenticity into Orlando's theme-crazed dining scene. A brief tour of ethnic eateries might include *ropa vieja*, paella, sweet fried plantains, and other Cuban specialties at **El Bohio** (5756 Dahlia Drive, tel: 407-282-1723) or **Rolando's** (870 East State Road, Casselberry, tel: 407-767-9677); pad thai and delicate spring rolls at **Royal Thai** (1202 North Semoran Boulevard, tel: 407-275-0776) or **Siam Garden** (1111 West Webster Avenue, Winter Park, tel: 407-599-7443); savory tandoori and samosas at **Far Pavilion Indian Cuisine** (5748 International Drive, tel: 407-351-5522) or **Memories of India** (7625 Turkey Lake Road, tel: 407-370-3277); tangy barbecue at **Bubbalou's Bodacious BBQ** (1471 Lee Road, Winter Park, tel: 407-628-1212) or **Sonny's Real Pit Bar-B-Q** (3390 University Boulevard, Winter Park, tel: 407-671-2002); hearty Mexican at **Taquitos Jalisco** (1041 South Dillard Street, Winter Garden, tel: 407-654-0363) and **PR's Restaurant** (499 West Fairbanks Avenue, Winter Park, tel: 407-645-2225.

Drinking and dining alfresco on Orange Street, downtown Orlando

Dinner Theater

Another popular option is dinner theater. Actually, *theater* is a misnomer. Most of the shows are more extravagant than a mere stage play, and some – like murder mystery dinners – involve a great deal of audience participation.

Don't expect a gourmet feast. The menus are limited, the food mass-produced. The most satisfying dishes are usually the simplest.

Among the best dinner shows in town is **Arabian Nights** (6225 US 192, tel: 407-239-9223), which stars 50 Arabian, Lippizaner, palomino, and quarter horses that are put through their paces by skilled riders. There's a plot involving

The sushi bar at Wolfgang Puck, Downtown Disney

the marriage of a sultan's daughter, but the real attractions are the stunt riders, expertly trained horses, and wisecracking emcee. Dinner includes a choice of chicken, prime rib, and lasagna and all the beer, wine, and soda you can drink.

Horses are also part of the show at **Medieval Times Dinner and Tournament** (4510 US 192, tel: 800-229-8300), where you cheer jousting knights while eating whole chicken or prime rib with your fingers.

The fantasy continues at **Pirates Dinner Adventure** (6400 Carrier Drive, tel: 407-248-0590), a swash-buckling romp played out on an elaborate set, with swordplay, aerialists, singalongs, slapstick, and a cast of swarthy buccaneers. Dinner includes chicken or beef barbecued on a pirate sword.

Masters of Magic (8815 International Drive, tel: 407-352-3456) is an extravagant magic show, in which the star, Typhoon Lou, does stagey illusions – levitation, vanishing, lady-sawed-in-half – and convincing close-up magic. Calling this a dinner show is a bit of a stretch. The meal consists of all the pizza and salad you can eat.

The audience is part of the entertainment at **Sleuth's**

> Dress is casual at all but the fanciest restaurants. A light sweater may come in handy even in summer, when air conditioning can be chilly.

Mystery Show and Dinner (Republic Square, 7508 Universal Boulevard, tel: 407-363-1985), where guests try to solve a who-dunnit by questioning the actors. Dinner includes a rather uninspired choice of Cornish hen, prime rib, or lasagna. The concept is similar, but the food is much better at the **MurderWatch Mystery Theater** in the Grosvenor Resort Hotel (1850 Hotel Plaza Boulevard, 407-827-6534); unfortunately, the show plays only on Saturday night.

Less successful is the amateurish **Capone's Dinner & Show** (4740 US 192, tel: 407-397-2378), ostensibly a party for Al Capone staged in a 1930s speakeasy. Cafeteria-style lasagna, ziti, spaghetti, and chicken may leave you as flat as the acting.

Romantic Restaurants

Trying to rekindle the old flame? If so, you might consider this abbreviated list of the Orlando area's most romantic restaurants:

Delfino Riviera (Portofino Bay Hotel, tel: 407-503-3463). Exquisite Ligurian cuisine in an atmosphere reminiscent of a Renaissance palazzo.

California Grill (Contemporary Resort, tel: 407-939-3463). Understated elegance overlooking Magic Kingdom fireworks.

Manuel's on the 28th (390 North Orange Avenue, tel: 407-246-6580). Dazzling vistas complement artful presentation at this downtown favorite.

Victoria & Albert's (Grand Floridian Resort, tel: 407-824-1089). Disney's version of a Victorian fantasy, featuring a seven-course dinner, a lavish setting, and formal service.

Chalet Suzanne Restaurant (3800 Chalet Suzanne Drive, Lake Wales, tel: 863-676-6011). Six-course candelit dinners at a classic Southern inn overlooking tiny Lake Suzanne.

Sci-Fi Dine-In Theater Restaurant (Disney-MGM Studios, tel: 407-939-3463). Remember smooching in the back seat of the family Chevy? Relive the magic at this theme park restaurant, where the 1950s drive-in theme is wonderful and the food is, well, not.

HANDY TRAVEL TIPS

An A–Z Summary of Practical Information

A

ACCOMMODATIONS (See also the list of RECOMMENDED HOTELS starting on page 125)

Your first decision is whether or not to stay at Disney World. You'll pay more for a hotel in 'the World,' but there are perks – proximity to the parks, free transportation, tickets for after-hours 'E-ride nights' at the Magic Kingdom and, perhaps the biggest draw, 24-hour immersion in the Disney experience. Universal offers an even juicier plum: guests at on-site resorts enjoy express access to nearly all Universal attractions.

Lodging outside the theme parks ranges from lavish resorts with every conceivable amenity to budget chain motels. You'll find the latter clustered along US 192 in Kissimmee a short drive from Disney World.

Traveling without reservations is ill-advised. Book several months ahead if you have your heart set on a particular hotel or if you want to stay at Disney World or Universal. Room rates vary enormously between the high season and the off season. Peak periods in Orlando are: Thanksgiving weekend, from Christmas to New Year's Day, Easter Week, Presidents week in February, spring break (the third week of March through the third week of April), and summer break.

Combined sales and bed tax is 11 percent in Orlando, 12 percent in Kissimmee.

AIRPORTS

Orlando International Airport (MCO) is large, modern, and easy to negotiate. Located about a 30-minute drive south of Orlando and east of Disney World, the airport services more than 25 million passengers annually, with non-stop or direct service to some 68 US cities and 25 international gateways. Passengers on domestic flights should check in at least 2 hours before departure. International passengers should arrive 3 hours before departure. Allow plenty of time to take the monorail shuttle from the core area, which has check-in and baggage claim, to the departure gates. More than two dozen car rental agencies operate at or near the airport (courtesy shuttles available). Taxis cost about $50 to Disney World, $45 to Kissimmee, and $30 to downtown Orlando and International Drive. Shuttle vans operated by Mears Transportation (tel: 407-423-5566) run about every 30 minutes and cost $16 to Disney World, $22 to Kissimmee, and $14 to downtown Orlando and International Drive. Limousine service is provided by Town & Country Transportation (tel: 407-828-3035). Lynx (tel: 407-841-8240) runs public buses from the airport to downtown Orlando. The ride takes about 40 minutes and costs $1.

B

BUDGETING FOR YOUR TRIP

To give you an idea of what to expect, here's a list of average prices in US dollars. These prices are only approximate. Orlando is an expensive city, but it is possible to have fun on a budget.

Hotels. This will be your major expense. For a double room (before tax), expect to pay $50–$100 per night for a budget room, $100–$200 a night for a moderate room, $200–$300 a night for an expensive room, and over $350 for a luxury room.

Meals. Restaurant prices vary widely depending on where you eat. If you're traveling cheaply, you can get a decent dinner at Denny's, Applebee's, or one of the other family chains for $10 or less; breakfast, of course, is even cheaper. Dinner at a moderate restaurant ranges between $15 and $25 per person. Fine restaurants generally cost $30 or more – often much more. A glass of wine is rarely less than $5, and a bottle is considered cheap at $15. Restaurants at the theme parks are significantly more expensive than those in the 'real world.' If you're watching your budget, eat before you enter and after you leave the parks and carry a few snacks in a backpack (coolers are not permitted) for sustenance during your visit.

Transportation. Public transportion within Disney World is free. If you're staying at a Disney resort, there's no need to rent a car except for the extra convenience, which is considerable. If you plan on venturing outside Disney World, a car is essential. Weekly rental of a mid-size vehicle runs $290–$320. Auto insurance costs up to $250 a week, depending on the level of coverage you select.

Theme parks. Admission options at Disney World can be confusing. At this writing, a one-park/one-day admission for visitors 10 and older is $50 (prices do not include tax). If you plan on visiting for more than two or three days and want the flexibility to enter more than one park per day, opt for a Park Hopper or Park Hopper Plus Pass. The Park Hopper includes unlimited admission to the Magic Kingdom, Epcot, Disney-MGM Studios, and Animal Kingdom and is available for 4 or 5 days. Park Hopper Plus includes all of the above plus admission to Pleasure Island, the water parks, and Wide World of Sports and is available for 5 to 7 days. By way of comparison, a 5-day Park Hopper Pass purchased at the gate is $230. A 5-day Park Hopper Plus Pass is $259. You'll save about 5 percent by purchasing the tickets in advance online <www.disneyworld.com> or by phone (tel: 407-934-7639). The passes do not need to be used on consecutive days, and there is no expiration on unused days. If you're staying at a Disney hotel, you can also opt for an Ultimate Park Hopper Pass, which entitles you to unlimited admission to all parks and attractions and can be used as a credit card within Disney World. In most cases, however, the added benefits don't offset the extra fee.

If you're visiting Disney World for more than 7 days or plan to return within a year, consider buying an Annual Pass ($369) to the four major theme parks or a Premium Annual Pass ($489) to the four parks plus Pleasure Island, DisneyQuest, Wide World of Sports, and all water parks.

The choices at Universal (tel: 407-363-8000) aren't quite as complicated. A one-day/one-park pass for visitors 10 and older is $50; a one-day/two-park pass is $75. A two-day/two-park pass is $95 and includes a third day free within one week of your first visit.

If you plan on spending more than three days at Universal, the best deal is a 5-day Bonus Pass for $90. One hitch: it's sold only online (<tickets.universalstudios.com>) and must be used on consecutive days.

The best deal in Orlando is the 4-Park Flex Ticket, which costs $170 and includes admission to Universal Studios, Islands of Adventure, CityWalk, SeaWorld, and Wet 'n Wild for 14 consecutive days. A 5-Park Flex Ticket costs $203 and covers all of the the above plus admission to Busch Gardens Tampa Bay.

One-day adult admission to SeaWorld and Busch Gardens is $50. Look for special deals on the Web <www.buschgardens.com> including, at press time, a second day free at SeaWorld with online ticket purchase.

C

CAR RENTAL/HIRE (See also DRIVING)

A car is essential if you want to explore Orlando outside Disney World. We strongly recommend that you make your reservation for a car rental before you leave home. You will need a driver's license and a major credit card (or be willing to put up a hefty cash deposit). The minimum age for renting a car is 21. Many companies impose an extra fee on drivers under 25.

CHILDCARE

You can have an adults-only night even if you're traveling with kids. Disney offers several childcare centers – they're called 'kids clubs' – for children ages 4 to 12. Most are open from 4.30pm to midnight. The fee is $10 an hour for each child and includes dinner. Call (407) 939-3463 for reservations.

Universal's on-site hotels have similar facilities for children ages 4 to 14. The fees here are $10 per hour for the first child, $8 per hour for each additional child in the same family; dinner is $10 extra. Hours are 5pm–11pm Sun–Thur, 5pm–midnight Fri–Sat. Call the hotels directly for reservations.

Travelers staying elsewhere in Orlando can arrange in-room babysitting by calling Kids' Night Out (tel: 407-827-5444). All babysitters are 18 or older and have undergone a background check and CPR training. Fees are $13.50 per hour for one child, $15.50 for two children, $17.50 for three, and $19.50 for four. There is a 4-hour minimum and a transportation fee of $8.

CLIMATE

Winter is usually delightful in central Florida, but there are rainy days and cold spells; temperatures occasionally approach freezing. On the other hand, winter temperatures can reach 80°F (30°C). Summer ranges from hot to very hot, with temperatures hovering around 90°F (32°C) with extreme humidity. Sudden, brief downpours and lightning storms occur almost every day from June to October; be prepared with an umbrella or rain poncho. For a weather report, dial (407) 824-4104 or log onto <b.orlandoweather.com>. Here are monthly average maximum and minimum daytime temperatures:

	J	F	M	A	M	J	J	A	S	O	N	D
°F	70	72	76	81	88	90	90	90	88	83	76	70
	49	54	56	63	67	74	74	74	74	67	58	52
°C	21	22	24	27	31	32	32	32	31	28	24	21
	9	12	13	17	19	23	23	23	23	19	14	11

CLOTHING

Casual lightweight clothing is the norm in Orlando, and most attractions permit shorts and sportswear. There is little need for formal attire, except at such fine restaurants as Victoria & Albert's, the Boheme and Manuel's on the 28th. Even at these places, ties are optional. A light raincoat (ponchos are sold at the theme parks) or an umbrella is advisable in summer. A light sweater comes in handy when air conditioning is too chilly. Most visitors walk 4 to 8 miles (6–13km) during a typical day at a theme park, so comfortable shoes are a must. The Florida sun is unmerciful, so wear a hat and sunglasses, and use plenty of sunscreen. A fanny pack or small backpack is also useful for stowing water bottles, snacks, souvenirs, and, if you intend to do water rides, a towel and a change of clothes

COMPLAINTS

Staff members at Disney World and Universal Orlando are trained to be responsive to the needs of guests. If you have a serious problem or feel strongly you've been wronged or treated unfairly, ask to speak to a manager and stick to your guns. More often than not, they will make a genuine effort to rectify the situation. For complaints or problems that don't have an on-the-spot solution, contact Walt Disney World Guest Communications, PO Box 10040, Lake Buena Vista, FL 32830-0040, e-mail: <wdw.guest.communications@disneyworld.com>; or Universal Orlando Guest Services, 1000 Universal Studios Plaza, Orlando, FL 32819, tel: (407) 224-6350. Success is less likely after your trip, so try to address difficulties before you leave.

If you have reason to complain about retail stores or business practices outside the theme parks, try to resolve the problem directly with the establishment in question. If that doesn't work, contact the Community Relations Manager, Orlando/Orange County Convention & Visitors Bureau, 6700 Forum Drive, Suite 100, Orlando, FL 32821, tel: (407) 354-5530.

CRIME (See also EMERGENCIES)

The big theme parks have their own security personnel. They are so discreet that you are hardly aware of their presence, but they'll be on hand if you need them. Walt Disney World is among the safest environments on Earth, but – as always – you should look after your property and keep in mind a few commonsense precautions:

- Always lock your hotel room door, and never admit any unauthorized person.
- Deposit valuables in a hotel safe.
- Never carry large amounts of cash; wear a minimum of jewelry.
- Carry as much money as possible in the form of travelers' checks, and keep a record of these (and your passport) separate from the checks, or simply use your ATM card, withdrawing only as much cash as you'll need for the day.
- If you are robbed, don't play the hero. Hand over what you have, then report it to the police immediately (tel: 911). Your insurance company will need to see a copy of the police report. For stolen or lost travelers' checks and credit cards, report the matter at once to the issuer so that payments can be stopped immediately.

CUSTOMS AND ENTRY REQUIREMENTS
(See also AIRPORTS)

Canadians need only provide evidence of their nationality. Citizens of the UK, Australia, New Zealand, and the Republic of Ireland no longer need a visa for stays of less than 90 days, just a valid passport and a return airline ticket. The airline will issue a visa waiver form. Citizens of South Africa need a visa – check with your local US consulate or embassy and allow three weeks for delivery.

You will be asked to complete a customs declaration form before you arrive in the US. Restrictions are as follows: You are generally allowed to bring in a reasonable quantity of tobacco and alcohol for your personal use. A non-resident may claim, free of duty and taxes, articles up to $100 in value for use as gifts for other persons. The exemption is valid only if the gifts accompany you, you stay 72 hours or more, and have not claimed this exemption within the preceding six months. Up to 100 cigars may be included within this gift exemption (Cuban cigars, however, are forbidden and may be confiscated). Arriving and departing passengers must report any money or checks, etc., exceeding a total of $10,000.

D

DRIVING (See also CAR RENTAL/HIRE)

Driving conditions. Driving is by far the easiest way to explore the Orlando area beyond Disney World, allowing you to zip quickly between the major parks, unless of course you encounter one of the many traffic jams that snarl the area's major arteries. If possible, avoid driving the I-4 corridor during rush hour. The speed limit on most highways in Florida is 65mph (105kph), though it's apt to be 55mph (90kph) or slower in congested areas or construction zones. The use of a seat belt is mandatory. Before leaving home, determine whether your own insurance will cover you when you're driving a rented car; if it does, you may not need to purchase car rental insurance.

Parking. Theme parks charge for parking unless you're staying at an on-site hotel or have a special pass. The parking lots are huge, so remember to note the section or space number before leaving your car.

Gas (petrol). Service stations are numerous and easy to find in the Orlando area, and many are open 24 hours a day. Pumping your own gas saves a few cents per gallon; some stations don't even have a full-service option. Remember to fill your rental car before returning it in order to avoid the agency's top-off charge.

Breakdowns and insurance. If you intend to do a lot of driving, consider joining the American Automobile Association (AAA). The fees are reasonable, and the benefits include emergency road service, maps, insurance and travelers' checks. AAA also offers discounts on admission to Disney and Universal theme parks, SeaWorld, Busch Gardens, Cypress Gardens, the Kennedy Space Center, and many other attractions. AAA has reciprocity agreements with many foreign automobile associations. For membership, log on to <www.aaasouth.com> or call (800) 222-1134. For emergency road service, call (800) 222-4357.

E

ELECTRICITY

110-volt 60-cycle AC is standard throughout the US. Plugs are the flat, parallel two-pronged variety. Foreign visitors without dual-voltage appliances will need a transformer and adapter plug.

EMBASSIES AND CONSULATES

Few English-speaking countries maintain a consulate in Florida. The nearest ones are listed below:

Australia: 630 Fifth Avenue, Suite 420, New York, NY 10111, tel: (212) 408-8400.

Canada: 200 South Biscayne Boulevard, Suite 1600, Miami, FL 33131, tel: (305) 579-1600.

New Zealand: Embassy, 37 Observatory Circle, Washington, DC 20008, tel: (202) 328-4800.

Republic of Ireland: 345 Park Avenue, 17th Floor, New York, NY 10022, tel: (212) 319-2555.

South Africa: 333 East 38th Street, 9th Floor, New York, NY 10016, tel: (212) 213-4880.

United Kingdom: 245 Peachtree Street Center Avenue, Atlanta, GA 20303, tel: (404) 524-5856.

EMERGENCIES (See also HEALTH AND MEDICAL CARE AND POLICE)

All-purpose emergency number: 911

EXPRESS ACCESS/FASTPASS

The biggest gripe about theme parks is the long lines. Both Disney and Universal have heard your grumbles and now offer programs that reduce the amount of time you'll spend staring at the back of another person's head. The cornerstone of this effort is an electronic system that allows visitors to reserve a ride on the most popular attractions. Disney calls the system Fastpass, Universal calls it Universal Express, but they work essentially the same way: You stick your ticket into a kiosk stationed near the attraction and choose a riding time. When you return, you'll be directed to an express lane. The maximum wait is usually 15 to 20 minutes, often less. If you don't mind splitting up your party, you can also take advantage of single rider lines, which offer time savings similar to the express system without having to return later.

G

GAY AND LESBIAN TRAVELERS

Each June Orlando and its theme parks are host to Gay Days. This event attracts over 100,000 gay and lesbian people along with their friends and families. Special events are held at Disney World, Universal Studios, and throughout Orlando. For more information on Gay Days, gay nightclubs, and other events, contact Gay and Lesbian Community Services, 714 East Colonial Drive, Orlando, FL 32803, tel: (407) 843-4297 or log onto Gay Orlando (<www.gayorlando.com>).

GETTING THERE

Orlando International Airport is large, modern and efficiently run. Several major US airlines offer direct flights to Orlando, including American, Delta, Continental, US Airways, and Northwest, as do such discount carriers as ATA, Jet Blue, Spirit, and Southwest. From the UK, Orlando is serviced by British Airways and Virgin Atlantic; from continental Europe by Iberia, LTU, MartinAir, and others; from Japan by ANA; from Canada by Air Canada; and from Mexico by AeroMexico.

Amtrak runs three lines to Orlando: the Silver Service, which starts in New York City and runs along the East Coast; the Sunset Limited, which departs from Los Angeles and runs through the Southwest and along the Gulf Coast; and the Auto Train, which transports passengers and their cars from Lorton, Virginia (near Washington DC) to Sanford, Florida (north of Orlando).

GUIDES AND TOURS

Disney World, Universal, and SeaWorld offer a wide range of behind-the-scenes tours, many limited to participants 16 or older. Tours range in price, frequency, and duration. Some require the purchase of separate park admission, and all require advance reservations. Among the most popular programs at Disney World (tel: 407-939-8687) are:

Backstage Magic. Behind the scenes at Epcot, Disney-MGM's animation studio and the underground 'utilidors' of the Magic Kingdom.

Gardens of the World. A botanical tour of Epcot.

Inside Animation. A look at the making of an animated film at Disney-MGM Studios.

Backstage Safari. Tour the animal-care facilities at Animal Kingdom.

Behind the Seeds. A walking tour of Epcot's Living with the Land pavilion, including the experimental greenhouse.

Dolphins in Depth. Explore the dolphin-care facility at Epcot's Livings Seas pavilion.

DiveQuest. Scuba diving in the Living Seas aquarium at Epcot. Participants must have scuba certification.

Keys to the Kingdom. Backstage tour of the Magic Kingdom.

Undiscovered Future World Tour. A behind-the-scenes tour of the Future World pavilions and the production of IllumiNations.

Universal offers VIP **Tours** of one or both parks, giving participants a glimpse of operational facilities and express access to several attractions. Call (407) 363-8295 for more information.

Options at SeaWorld (tel: 407-370-1382 or 407-363-2380) include:

Trainer for a Day. Work side-by-side with SeaWorld trainers as they conduct behavioral routines and care for dolphins and seals.

False Killer Whale Interaction Program. Face-to-face encounters with these unusual marine mammals.

Animal Care Experience. Firsthand lessons in the rescue and rehabilitation of injured manatees and the care of captive seals, walruses, and beluga whales.

Sharks Deep Dive. Scuba dive or snorkel with sharks.

H

HEALTH AND MEDICAL CARE

The US has a good but expensive health-care system, and Orlando has several excellent hospitals. Payment for any medical services will be expected on the spot. It is wise to arrange for health and accident insurance before your visit, either through a travel agency or an insurance company.

In the case of illness or injury, your hotel should be able to provide a list of doctors. If you need to be seen immediately, go directly to the emergency ward of the nearest hospital. For emergency ambulance and EMTs, call 911.

Pharmacies. It is generally advisable to bring with you any medicines you require regularly. Be aware that many medicines you can buy over the counter in your home country require a prescription in the US. If you need prescription drugs during your stay, you will have to get a prescription from a local physician.

HOLIDAYS

The following are national holidays in the US. Banks, post offices, and government offices are closed on these days. The major theme parks are open 365 days a year.

New Year's Day	January 1
Martin Luther King Day	Third Monday in January
President's Day	Third Monday in February
Memorial Day	Last Monday in May
Independence Day	July 4
Labor Day	First Monday in September
Columbus Day	Second Monday in October
Veterans' Day	November 11
Thanksgiving Day	Fourth Thursday in November
Christmas Day	December 25

L

LAUNDRY AND DRY CLEANING

Self-service laundries are located throughout Orlando; ask at your hotel – some even have self-service facilities on-site. Dry-cleaners are also widely available and reasonably priced. Better hotels offer 24-hour dry cleaning service.

LOST PROPERTY

Each theme park maintains a lost and found. Here are the numbers:
Disney World, tel: (407) 824-4245
Universal Studios, tel: (407) 224-6355
Islands of Adventure, tel: (407) 224-4245
SeaWorld, tel: (407) 351-3600 (ext. 3415)

M

MEDIA

Radio and Television. Almost all hotel rooms have cable television, although most charge a fee to view a selection of first-run movies. There are about 36 local AM and FM radio stations operating in the Orlando area. Traffic reports, weather, and news are broadcast regularly on WTKS-FM 104.1, WDBO-AM 580, WWNZ-AM 740, WOTS-AM 1220 and WTRR-AM 1400.

Magazines and Newspapers. The daily *Orlando Sentinel* covers central Florida. The Friday Calendar section has listings of area events. The *Orlando Weekly* specializes in alternative news, dining, and entertainment. *Orlando Magazine* is a glossy monthly publication with feature articles, restaurant reviews, and a calendar of events. Newsstands, convenience stores, and grocery stores also carry the *Miami Herald* and other Florida newspapers, as well as national papers such as *USA Today*, the *Wall Street Journal*, and *New York Times*. Foreign newspapers and magazines are more difficult to come by, though you can usually find a select few at large bookstores and newsstands.

MONEY

Currency. The dollar is divided into 100 cents. The coins are as follows: 1¢ (penny), 5¢ (nickel), 10¢ (dime), 25¢ (quarter), and $1 (new in 2000). Bank notes of $1, $5, $10, $20, $50, and $100 are common, but some establishments will not accept denominations over $20 unless you make an especially large purchase.

Credit cards. Visa, MasterCard, American Express, Discover, and other major cards are widely accepted. Some credit/debit cards can be used to withdraw cash from ATMs. Call your credit card company or bank for more information.

Exchange facilities. Currency exchange offices are few and far between in the US, even in tourist centers like Orlando. You'll find exchange offices at the airport, the major theme parks (ask for Guest Services), large hotels and banks. Rates and fees vary. In general, you'll get the most favorable rate by withdrawing cash from an ATM or making purchases with a credit card.

ATMs. These are widely available. However, most banks charge non-depositors a fee to use their ATMs.

Sales tax. There is no VAT in the US. A sales tax of 6 percent in Orange County and 7 percent in Osceola and Seminole Counties is added to the marked price of all goods, including clothing and some food items. Visitors also pay a 5 percent bed tax.

Travelers' checks. It is wise to buy travelers' checks denominated in US$. Foreign currency travelers' checks must be exchanged before using them for purchases in the US.

O

OPEN HOURS

Theme parks. Hours change seasonally, sometimes daily. Call ahead for a schedule.
Banks. Mon–Fri 9am–3pm; many are open Sat 9am–2pm.
Offices. 9am–5pm is the norm for business offices.
Stores. Most stores are open Mon–Sat 10am–6pm.
Restaurants. Most restaurants are open until 10pm or 11pm during the week, and until midnight or later on Friday and Saturday.

ORIENTATION

Getting your bearings in the Orlando area is fairly easy. The main corridor is a 20-mile (32-km) stretch of I-4 that runs from downtown Orlando to Disney World. In between are most of the area's major attractions, including Universal, SeaWorld, and International Drive. Kissimmee, a popular gateway to the Orlando area with several attractions of its own, is a few miles southeast of Disney World via US 192. Orlando International Airport is approximately 18 miles (29km) east of Disney World and 10 miles (16km) southeast of downtown Orlando.

P

PHOTOGRAPHY AND VIDEO

All popular brands of film and photographic equipment are available. Pre-recorded videotapes bought in the US will not work in Europe. Tapes can be converted, but at considerable expense.

POLICE (See also CRIME AND EMERGENCIES)

In an emergency, dial 911. For other matters, dial local police departments directly: Orlando (407) 246-4155, Kissimmee (407) 847-0176, Winter Garden (407) 656-3636. The major theme parks maintain their own security personnel. Ask any attendant for assistance.

POST OFFICES

Post offices are usually open weekdays 8am–5pm, Sat 9am–1pm. A domestic letter costs 37¢, a domestic postcard 23¢, an overseas postcard 70¢. You can often buy stamps at the reception desk in your hotel, from stamp machines and, of course, at a post office.

PUBLIC TRANSPORTATION (See also AIRPORTS)

Bus. Lynx offers public bus services, throughout the Orlando area. Call (407) 841-2279 or log onto <www.golynx.com> for route information. Adult fare is $1, with free transfers for up to 90 minutes. Exact change is required. A weekly pass is $10. A bus service called Lymmo, also run by Lynx, operates in downtown Orlando. I Ride trolleys operate along International Drive. Many hotels offer free shuttles to major attractions, which are often more convenient than public transportation.

Taxis. Taxis are usually available at all theme parks and large hotels. When in doubt, ask a hotel desk clerk to call for a pickup.

R

RESTROOMS

Public bathrooms are well-maintained at nearly all tourist attractions. If you need a bathroom while traveling between destinations, try a service station. Restaurants sometimes restrict restrooms to paying customers, but fast-food joints like McDonald's or Burger King rarely enforce restrictions.

T

TELEPHONE/FAX

Telephones. You can dial information (411) or an operator (dial 0) for free from any pay phone. All numbers with an 800, 888, or 877 prefix are toll-free. For domestic long-distance calls in the US, dial 1 +

the area code + the 7-digit number. For international calls, dial 011 + the country code + the number.

The area code in the Orlando area is 407. Area code 321 is an 'overlay' for the area and will be assigned to new numbers as the 407 area code is exhausted.

Local calls cost 25¢ for the first three minutes, after which the operator will tell you to add more money. Most convenience stores sell calling cards for long-distance calls. You may wish to avoid the hefty surcharges some hotels add to outgoing calls by using a calling card and a pay phone.

Fax. A fax can be sent from almost any Orlando hotel, though you may find less expensive fees at Kinko's and other copy shops.

TIME ZONES

Orlando is on Eastern Standard Time. In spring (between April and October) Daylight Saving Time is adopted and clocks move ahead one hour. The following chart shows the time in various cities in winter:

Los Angeles	**Orlando**	London	Paris	Sydney
9am	noon	5pm	6pm	4am

TIPPING

A tip of 15 percent is customary at bars and restaurants. Some restaurants will include a gratuity in your bill, especially if you are dining with a large party. In general, porters are tipped $1–2 per bag; cloakroom attendants and doormen who find you a taxi, $2–3; valet parking attendants, $2–3; taxi drivers and hairdressers, 15–20 percent.

TOURIST INFORMATION

Kissimmee/St Cloud Convention & Visitors Bureau, 1925 Bill Beck Boulevard, Kissimmee, FL 34744, tel: (407) 847-5000.
Orlando/Orange County Convention & Visitors Bureau, 6700 Forum Drive, Suite 100, FL 32821, tel: (407) 363-5800.

SeaWorld Orlando, 7007 SeaWorld Drive, Orlando, FL 32821, tel: (407) 351-3600.

Universal Orlando, 1000 Universal Studios Plaza, Orlando, FL 32819, tel: (407) 363-8000.

Walt Disney World, PO Box 10000, Lake Buena Vista, FL 32830-1000, tel: (407) 934-7639.

Winter Park Chamber of Commerce, Box 280, Winter Park, FL 32790, tel: (407) 644-8281.

TRAVELERS WITH DISABILITIES

When it comes to accessibility for people with disabilities, Disney World and Orlando are ahead of the curve. Most buses, the monorail, and most water launches are equipped for wheelchairs as are public restrooms and most restaurants and hotels. Wheelchairs and motorized carts (also known as electronic convenience vehicles or ECVs) are available for rent in limited numbers at the theme parks, usually just inside the entrance. Some attractions can be boarded in a wheelchair. Others can be boarded only by transferring out of a wheelchair and into the ride's seat. Staff members are not permitted to help with the transfer, so a companion must be present to assist you. Most stores are accessible but are often crowded with merchandise and people.

Disney, Universal, and SeaWorld also offer captioning systems, amplification devices and/or printed scripts for guests with hearing impairments. Guides fluent in sign language can be arranged with advanced notice. Telephones equipped with TDD or TTY are available; consult a guidemap for locations. Audio cassettes and tape recorders are available free of charge to visitors with impaired sight; inquire at guest relations.

For more information, call well in advance of your trip: Disney World (407) 939-7807, Universal Orlando (407) 224-6350, SeaWorld (407) 363-2414. Both Disney World and Universal publish a guidebook for visitors with disabilities. Request a free copy at guest relations near the park entrances.

W

WEBSITES

Several websites will prove useful when planning your trip:
The Orlando/Orange County Convention & Visitors Bureau <www.orlandoinfo.com> provides information on a wide variety of topics, including lodging, dining, attractions, and transportation as well as tips on discounts and travel packages. At <www.orlandotouristinfo rmationbureau.com>, you'll find general travel information and links to an airline booking service. For good deals on lodging and transportation, try <www.go2orlando.com>.

Three publications maintain websites with local news, restaurant reviews, and information on the arts, tourist attractions, and upcoming events: The *Orlando Weekly* <www.orlandoweekly.com>, *Orlando Sentinel* <www.orlandosentinel.com>, and *Orlando Magazine* <www.orlandomagazine.com>.

Here are websites of some of the main attractions:
Busch Gardens <www.4adventure.com/buschgardens/fla/>
Cypress Gardens <www.cypressgardens.com>
Gatorland <www.gatorland.com>
Harry P. Leu Gardens <www.leugardens.org>
Holy Land Experience <www.theholylandexperience.com>
Kennedy Space Center <www.kennedyspacecenter.com>
Orange County Regional History Center <www.thehistorycenter.org>
Orlando Museum of Art <www.omart.org>
SeaWorld Orlando <www.buschgardens.com/seaworld/fla/>
Splendid China <www.floridasplendidchina.com>
Universal Orlando <www.universalstudios.com>
Walt Disney World <www.disneyworld.com>

WEIGHTS AND MEASURES

The US is one of the few countries in the world that doesn't use the metric system.

Recommended Hotels

Sleeping with Mickey – that is, staying at a Disney World hotel – has advantages, but you'll pay a premium for the privilege. There's free transportation to the theme parks, proximity to Disney restaurants, and access to after-hours 'E-ride nights' at the Magic Kingdom. Not to be outdone, Universal offers the juiciest perk: guests at its hotels enjoy express access to nearly all the attractions at the theme parks.

You'll save a considerable sum for similar lodgings outside Disney, ranging from extravagant resorts and business-style hotels to modest chain motels. There are even a few small inns and boutique hotels, though they're few and far between. Substantial discounts are available at online services like <www.hoteldiscount.com>.

The following categories apply to the cost of a standard double room for one night and do not include tax:

$$$$$	over $400
$$$$	$300–400
$$$	$200–300
$$	$100–200
$	below $100

DISNEY WORLD

Animal Kingdom Lodge $$–$$$ *2901 Osceola Parkway, Lake Buena Vista 32830, tel: (407) 938-3000, fax: (407) 938-4799, <www.disneyworld.com>.* A four-story observation window in the lobby of this safari-style resort overlooks a 33-acre (13-hectare) savanna populated with giraffe, zebra, and other African animals. Large, comfortable rooms feature handcrafted furnishings; many have balconies with views of the wildlife. 1,293 rooms.

BoardWalk Inn and Villas $$$$–$$$$$ *2101 North Epcot Resorts Boulevard, Lake Buena Vista 32830, tel: (407) 939-5100, fax: (407) 939-5150, <www.disneyworld.com>.* A seaside theme prevails at this luxurious resort adjacent to Disney's BoardWalk, an entertainment complex set on Crescent Lake with stores, fine restaurants, and nightclubs recalling the atmosphere of Atlantic City *circa* 1925. Within walking distance (or a short boat ride) to Epcot and Disney-MGM Studios. 372 rooms, 520 villas.

Caribbean Beach Resort $$–$$$ *900 Cayman Way, Lake Buena Vista 32830, tel: (407) 934-3400, fax: (407) 934-3288, <www.disneyworld.com>.* A top-to-bottom renovation has restored the luster to the five 'tropical villages' encompassed by this brightly colored, palm-shaded resort near Epcot and Disney-MGM Studios. Guest rooms are housed in two-story buildings clustered around a 45-acre (18-hectare) lake, with beaches and boating. Rooms are large and comfortably furnished, though not extravagant. A good choice in the moderate price range. 2,112 rooms.

Contemporary Resort $$$–$$$$ *4600 North World Drive, Lake Buena Vista 32830, tel: (407) 824-1000, fax: (407) 824-3539, <www.disneyworld.com>.* Audaciously modern when it opened in 1971, this 15-story A-shaped pyramid now feels a bit dated, although seeing the monorail cruise through the atrium is still a kick. Tower rooms have gorgeous views of the Magic Kingdom. The California Grill, one of Disney's finest restaurants, is on the 15th floor. A convention center attracts business people. 1,030 rooms.

Coronado Springs Resort $$–$$$ *1000 West Buena Vista Drive, Lake Buena Vista 32830, tel: (407) 939-1000, fax: (407) 939-1003, <www.disneyworld.com>.* Mexico and the American Southwest provide stylistic cues for this sprawling resort arranged around a lake and encompassing four pools, including one with a water slide and a waterfall that cascades down a Mayan temple. An adjacent convention center attracts business clients, and the relatively moderate price lures families. Buses serve the parks. 1,920 rooms.

Disney's All-Star Sports, Music, and Movie Resorts $–$$ *1991 West Buena Vista Drive, Lake Buena Vista 32830, tel: (407) 939-5000 (Sports), -6000 (Music), -7000 (Movies), fax: (407) 939-*

7333 (Sports), 7222 (Music), 7111 (Movies), <www.disneyworld. com>. Disney's only budget accommodations are small motel-style rooms with a few over-the-top architectural touches like the giant guitars and football helmets that adorn the buildings. This may be a reasonable option if you're on a tight budget and don't intend to spend much time in your room. Otherwise, the spare amenities, sprawling layout (there are more than 30 three-story buildings), and hordes of overexcited children make this a poor choice. 5,760 rooms.

Grand Floridian Resort $$$$$ 4401 Grand Floridian Way, Lake Buena Vista 32830, tel: (407) 824-3000, fax: (407) 824-3186, <www.disneyworld.com>. This extravagant re-creation of a Victorian hotel is Disney at its most luxurious… and expensive. But then, this is what Disney does best – creating an environment where every detail, from the crystal chandeliers and open-cage elevators to the formal gardens and aviary, is in place. Rooms are spacious and sunny, with plush contemporary touches. Two of the five restaurants – Victoria and Albert's and Citricos – are among Disney World's finest. A full-service spa offers everything from a 30-minute massage to a full day of pampering. The monorail and water launches transport guests to the Magic Kingdom. 900 rooms and suites.

Old Key West Resort $$$–$$$$$ 1510 North Cove Road, Lake Buena Vista 32830, tel: (407) 827-7700, fax: (407) 827-7710, <www.disneyworld.com>. This cheery, tropical resort near Downtown Disney recalls the ambiance of Florida's southernmost city at the turn of the 20th century. Accommodations range from deluxe studios to three-bedroom villas, most with kitchens, balconies, or patios, and whirlpool tubs in the master bedroom. 709 villas.

Polynesian Resort $$$$–$$$$$ 1600 Seven Seas Drive, Lake Buena Vista 32830, tel: (407) 824-2000, fax: (407) 824-3174, <www.disneyworld.com>. Hawaii is the theme of this sprawling complex on the shores of Seven Seas Lagoon, directly across from the Magic Kingdom. The property features a lushly vegetated, skylit lobby, spacious rooms (many with balconies) with rattan furnishings, a sandy beach, and an expansive, palm-shaded pool with grottoes, waterfalls, and a water slide. A *luau* features Hawaiian dancing, roast pork, and other Polynesian specialties. The monorail and ferries transport guests to the Magic Kingdom. 850 rooms.

Walt Disney World Dolphin $$$$–$$$$$ *1500 Epcot Resorts Boulevard, Lake Buena Vista 32830, tel: (407) 934-4000, fax: (407) 934-4000, <www.swandolphin.com>.* **Walt Disney World Swan $$$$–$$$$$** *1200 Epcot Resorts Boulevard, Lake Buena Vista 32830, tel: (407) 934-3000, fax: (407) 934-4499, <www. swandol phin.com>.* Designed by noted architect Michael Graves and managed by Westin and Sheraton, respectively, this pair of hotels on either side of Crescent Lake is known for the gargantuan sculptures atop their roofs and for whimsical (some might say bizarre) contemporary decor. The rooms are slightly larger at the Dolphin and the pool here – an extravagant seashell-shaped affair with a waterfall and slide – is more elaborate than the Swan's. Ferries serve Epcot and Disney-MGM Studios. 2,270 rooms and suites.

Wilderness Lodge $$$–$$$$ *901 Timberline Drive, Lake Buena Vista 32830, tel: (407) 938-4300, fax: (407) 824-3232, <www.disneyworld.com>.* Inspired by the rustic elegance of America's grand National Park lodges, this eight-story lakefront lodge features a soaring stone-and-timber lobby and spacious guest rooms decorated with western-style art and furnishings. Villas, in a five-story adjoining complex, range from studios with kitchenettes to two-bedroom units with dining areas, kitchens, whirlpool tubs and VCRs. Artists Point, one of two restaurants, features the cuisine of the Pacific Northwest. An artificial geyser (a la Old Faithful) erupts periodically near a pool designed to look like a natural hot spring. Ferries connect the resort to the Magic Kingdom. 760 rooms and suites.

Yacht and Beach Club Resorts $$$–$$$$ *1700 Epcot Resorts Boulevard, Lake Buena Vista 32830, tel: (407) 934-7000, fax: (407) 934-3450, <www.disneyworld.com>.* Clapboard siding and nautical theming bring to mind the quaint seaside villages of New England at these adjacent resorts on Crescent Lake within walking distance of Epcot and Disney's BoardWalk. Standard rooms have either one king-size or two queen-size beds; one- to three-bedroom villas sleep up to eight. The resort's highlight is Stormalong Bay, a water park with whirlpools, slides and a beach. 1,213 rooms, 208 villas.

ELSEWHERE IN THE ORLANDO AREA

KISSIMMEE

Celebration Hotel $$$$ *700 Bloom Street, Celebration 34747, tel: (407) 566-6000, fax: (407) 566-6001, <www.celebrationhotel. com>.* Located in the Disney-designed town of Celebration, this elegant boutique hotel feels like a million miles away from Disney World, which is just next door. The peaceful terrace has rocking chairs and overlooks a pool and lake. Guest rooms have a classic Southern feeling, with pinstriped wallpaper, reproduction antique furnishings, CD players and high-speed Internet access; some have balconies. 115 rooms.

DoubleTree Resort Orlando – Villas at Maingate $$ *4787 West Irlo Bronson Highway, Kissimmee 34746, tel: (407) 397-0555, fax: (407) 397-1968, <www.doubletree.com>.* One-, two- and three-bedroom suites with kitchen, dining area, and living room are set on landscaped grounds a short drive from Disney World. A good value for a long stay or if you simply want extra room. 150 suites.

LAKE BUENA VISTA

Hyatt Regency Grand Cypress Resort $$$$ *1 Grand Cypress Boulevard, Orlando, 32836, tel: (407) 239-1234, fax: (407) 239-3800 <www.hyattgrandcypress.com>.* Encompassed within this beautifully landscaped, 1,500-acre (600-hectare) property are an equestrian center, three golf courses (including one designed by Jack Nicklaus), 12 tennis courts, a nature preserve, and an enormous swimming pool with a dozen waterfalls, secluded grottoes, and two water slides. Guest quarters range from comfortable standard rooms to multi-room suites in a complex of villas. Five restaurants run the gamut from haute cuisine to a lively saloon. 750 rooms and suites.

Marriott Orlando World Center $$$–$$$$ *8701 World Center Drive, Orlando 32821, tel: (407) 239-4200, fax: (407) 238-8777, <www.marriott.com>.* The grounds are exquisitely landscaped at this 200-acre (80-hectare) resort and convention center about 2 miles (3km) from Disney. Gardens, lakes, tennis courts, a health club, an 18-hole golf course, and several eateries (including an elegant Italian restaurant and Japanese steakhouse) are a few notable diversions. Generous rooms – all with balconies and pastel-toned decor – are in a 27-story tower and adjoining wing. 2,100 rooms and suites.

PerriHouse Bed & Breakfast Inn $$ *10417 Vista Oaks Court, Lake Buena Vista 32836, tel: 800-780-4830 or (407) 909-1469, fax: (407) 876-0241, <www.perrihouse.com>.* Set on a 2-acre bird sanctuary about 3 miles (5km) from Downtown Disney, this little inn is an island of serenity in a sea of commercial excess and a favorite of birdwatchers. Guest rooms are cheerful and homey, with four-poster beds and private baths. A small pool, Jacuzzi and complimentary breakfast round out the picture. 8 rooms.

UNIVERSAL ORLANDO

Hard Rock Hotel $$$–$$$$ *800 Universal Boulevard, Orlando 32819, tel: (407) 503-7625, fax: (407) 503-7655, <themeparks.universalstudios.com/orlando/website/resort_hotels/hotel_map.html>.* Rock 'n' roll memorabilia is exhibited throughout this luxurious Mission-style hotel, a short walk from Universal's theme parks. Accommodations range from standard rooms with queen-size beds to opulent suites with separate sitting areas. The complex overlooks an expansive, palm-shaded pool with a beach, water slide, underwater sound system, and outdoor bar. There are several lounges and restaurants, including the ritzy Palm steakhouse. 650 rooms and suites.

Portofino Bay Hotel $$$–$$$$$ *5601 Universal Boulevard, Orlando 32819, tel: (407) 503-1000; fax: (407) 503-1166, <themeparks.universalstudios.com/orlando/website/resort_hotels/hotel_map.html>.* Universal's most luxurious accommodations are housed in this re-creation of Portofino, Italy, complete with a picturesque harbor. Italian furnishings, marble tubs, comfy duvets, and sound systems are a few of the touches that create an elevated level of comfort. Some suites include the services of a butler. Facilities include elaborate pools, a full-service spa, restaurants and lounges. Gourmet dining is offered at the Delfino Riviera. 750 rooms and suites.

Royal Pacific Resort $$–$$$$ *6300 Hollywood Way, Orlando 32819, tel: (407) 503-3000, fax: (407) 503-3113, <themeparks.universalstudios.com/orlando/website/resort_hotels/hotel_map.html>.* Centered on a lagoon-like pool surrounded by cabanas, palm trees, a beach, and a waterfall, Universal's 'budget' hotel is inspired by the South Pacific. The theming is quite elaborate, though the rooms are smaller and more modestly furnished than those at other on-site hotels. Five restaurants, and lounges include the Tchoup Chop, an Asian eatery run by celebrity chef Emeril Lagasse.

INTERNATIONAL DRIVE

Arnold Palmer's Bay Hill Club & Lodge $$–$$$ *9000 Bay Hill Boulevard, Orlando 32819, tel: (407) 876-2429, fax: (407) 876-1035, <www.bayhill.com>.* Duffers are in heaven at this golf resort, where they can play two championship courses or brush up their techniques in the Arnold Palmer Golf Academy. The atmosphere at the wood-and-stone lodge is low-key and clubby, with nicely appointed rooms. Arnie is often in residence during the winter months. 58 rooms.

Castle DoubleTree Resort $$ *8629 International Drive, Orlando 32819, tel: (407) 345-1511, fax: (407) 248-8181, <www.doubletreecastle.com>.* Spires, mosaics, banners, and rich purple and gold drapes and bedspreads give this mid-range hotel a touch of medieval whimsy. Amenities include two restaurants, a fitness center, free shuttles to the theme parks, and a pleasant courtyard pool. 216 rooms.

Embassy Suites International Drive South $$ *8978 International Drive, Orlando 32819, tel: (407) 352-1400, fax: (407) 363-1120 <www.embassysuitesorlando.com>.* Want a little extra elbow room? Consider booking this all-suite hotel, where each unit has a bedroom and separate living room furnished in understated contemporary style. An atrium lobby trimmed out with Italian marble, waterfalls, and lush tropical gardens as well as a fitness room, two pools, free shuttles to Disney World, and a complimentary hot breakfast add to the property's considerable value. 245 suites.

Holiday Inn Family Suites Resort $$–$$$ *1800 International Drive, Orlando 32821, tel: (407) 387-5437, fax: (407) 387-1489, <www.hifamilysuites.com>.* Despite its name, this hotel has a lot to offer travelers without children. All suites have one or two bedrooms, a living area and a kitchenette; some are equipped with a 50-inch TV or exercise equipment. Newlyweds and other lovers should ask for the honeymoon suite. 800 suites.

Peabody Orlando $$–$$$$ *9801 International Drive, Orlando 32819, tel: (407) 352-4000, fax: (407) 363-1505, <www.peabody-orlando.com>.* It's a time-honored tradition. Every morning five ducks are paraded into the lobby of the Peabody Hotel, where they happily spend the day paddling in a marble fountain. Located across from the convention center and popular with both business and leisure travelers, the Peabody offers well-appointed rooms with contemporary furnishings. Three fine restaurants, live entertainment, a health club, and an Olympic-size pool are just a few of the many amenities. 890 rooms and suites.

Renaissance Orlando Resort $$–$$$ *6677 Sea Harbor Drive, Orlando 32821, tel: (407) 351-5555, fax: (407) 351-9991, <www.renaissancehotels.com>.* A grand, sunlit atrium with sleek glass elevators, goldfish ponds, and what appears to be acres of marble flooring set the tone for this 10-story tower and convention complex. Guest quarters are roomy, well-appointed and equally appealing to tourists and business travelers. The main restaurant, Atlantis, offers fine Continental dining. A coffee shop and deli are good for a quick breakfast or lunch. The location is ideal for those who want to explore several parks. The hotel is across the street from SeaWorld and about 15 minutes from Universal and Disney World. Amenities include a pool and an exercise room. 780 rooms.

DOWNTOWN ORLANDO

Courtyard at Lake Lucerne $–$$$ *211 North Lucerne Circle East, Orlando 32801, tel: (407) 648-5188, fax: (407) 246-1368, <www.orlandohistoricinn.com>.* Four historic houses, each of a different style, surround a courtyard overlooking Lake Lucerne, a short walk to restaurants and nightclubs. Guest rooms tend to reflect the house's overall style – Victorian, art deco, Edwardian, Southern – some with a sleigh or four-poster bed. 30 rooms.

Four Points Hotel Orlando $$ *151 East Washington Street, Orlando 32801, tel: (407) 841-3220, fax: (407) 648-4758, <www.starwood.com>.* Mediterranean style sets the tone for this hotel, whose low-key elegance suits travelers who want to avoid the hubbub around Disney and International Drive. Indulge yourself by asking for a suite with a view of Lake Eola. 250 rooms and suites.

Veranda Bed & Breakfast $$ *115 North Summerlin Avenue, Orlando 32801, tel: (407) 849-0321, fax: (407) 849-0321 ext. 28, <www.theverandabandb.com>.* Gracious Southern style is the hallmark of this inn, a complex of four historic buildings dating to the early 1900s and set in Thornton Park, within walking distance of restaurants and entertainment. The carriage house is particularly cozy. Continental breakfast is included. 12 rooms.

Westin Grand Bohemian $$–$$$ *325 South Orange Avenue, Orlando 32801, tel: (407) 313-9000, fax: (407) 313-9001, <www.grandbohemianhotel.com>.* A self-described 'Experience in Art and Music,' this Bohemian-themed hotel features more than 100 pieces of artwork, including drawings by Gustav Klimt and Egon Schiele. Guest rooms are furnished in dark Java wood tones, soft red and purple velvet, down comforters, and Tiffany-style lamps. The intimate Bosendorfer's Lounge (named after the rare Imperial Grand Bosendorfer piano) and elegant Boheme Restaurant are rapidly becoming favorites of downtown's business and arts community. Other amenities include a Starbucks coffee shop, outdoor pool, spa, and privileges at nearby Citrus Athletic Club. 250 rooms and suites.

Recommended Restaurants

Once derided as a culinary wasteland, Orlando has made impressive strides in recent years, thanks largely to a crew of hot young chefs who are staking a claim to one of the world's biggest tourist markets. Even food at the theme parks – notoriously mediocre – has taken a turn for the better, though you'll still pay through the nose for it.

The price categories are based on the average cost of a three-course meal for one person and do not include drinks or tip. Restaurants take major credit cards except where noted.

$$$$$	over $75
$$$$	$50–75
$$$	$35–50
$$	$25–35
$	below 25

DISNEY WORLD

Artist Point $$–$$$ *Wilderness Lodge, 901 West Timberline Drive, tel: (407) 939-3463.* Inspired by America's national-park lodges, this hotel restaurant features salmon, rainbow trout, elk chops, venison, bison, and other hearty dishes associated with the American West. The wine list features labels from the Pacific Northwest.

California Grill $$$ *Contemporary Resort, 4600 North World Drive, tel: (407) 939-3463.* Views of the Magic Kingdom are spectacular from this refined restaurant on the 15th floor of the Contemporary Resort. The menu changes seasonally but usually includes entrees like oak-roasted chicken and pork tenderloin prepared with a light California touch. Don't pass up the appetizers, an eclectic mix of sushi salads and pasta. Ask to be seated in time for the fireworks.

Les Chefs de France $$$ *Epcot, tel: (407) 939-3463.* Three renowned chefs – Paul Bocuse, Gaston Lenôtre, and Roger Vergé –

created and now supervise this classic French brasserie, regarded as one of the finest restaurants at Disney World.

Hollywood Brown Derby $$–$$$ *Disney-MGM Studios, tel: (407) 939-3463.* A re-creation of a legendary Hollywood eatery, this is one of Disney's most elegant theme-park restaurants, with snappily attired waiters, starched white linens, and a candlelit atmosphere. The menu changes often but usually features Cobb salad (invented at the original Brown Derby in the 1930s), filet mignon, rack of lamb and a variety of seafood and pasta dishes. The list of California wines is brief but sensible; the desserts are just short of sinful.

House of Blues $$ *Downtown Disney, tel: (407) 934-2583.* Jambalaya, etoufee, seafood gumbo, and bread pudding drizzled with brandy are a few of the Southern specialties at this surprisingly satisfying chain operation, dressed up like a Mississippi roadhouse. A top-notch lineup of musicians, ranging from crusty old bluesmen to heavy metal bands, perform in the adjoining concert hall, but the biggest treat may be the Sunday gospel brunch, which features an all-you-can eat Southern feast accompanied by a rousing gospel choir.

Planet Hollywood $$ *Downtown Disney, tel: (407) 827-7827.* Movie memorabilia crams every inch of this zany blue sphere, part of the international chain launched by Arnold Schwarzenegger, Bruce Willis, Sly Stallone, and entrepreneur Robert Earl. The food – hefty platters of burgers, sandwiches, steaks, and pasta – has improved since a 1999 brush with bankruptcy, though the line-up to be seated can be daunting, even with reservations.

Rainforest Cafe $$–$$$ *Animal Kingdom, tel: (407) 938-9100.* What looks like the side of a mountain with a huge waterfall gushing over the top is actually a restaurant with an elaborate jungle theme. Inside it's all leafy green foliage and animal calls. There's even a (simulated) thunderstorm. The food's pretty good, too, with dishes like coconut shrimp, pot roast, thick burgers, and 'rasta pasta' that make up in quantity what they lack in finesse. A second Rainforest Cafe – this one looks like a volcano – is at Downtown Disney.

Spoodles $–$$ *Disney's BoardWalk, tel: (407) 939-3463.* Mediterranean flavors are the focus of this open-kitchen restaurant, with specialties like Moroccan spiced tuna, grilled lamb chops, and wood-fired flat breads, and an appetizing *tapas* menu.

Victoria & Albert's $$$$$ *Grand Floridian Resort, 4401 Grand Floridian Way, tel: (407) 824-1089.* Disney spins a Victorian fantasy at this prix-fixe restaurant. The seven-course meal is served by a white-gloved butler and maid (Albert and Victoria) in a romantic domed dining room. The menu features some of the finest Continental cuisine in town. Very expensive but, fans say, worth the money.

Wolfgang Puck Cafe $$–$$$ *Downtown Disney, tel: (407) 938-9653.* The huge Orlando outpost of Puck's culinary empire draws a lively crowd eager to sample sushi, gourmet pizza, salads, steak, and seafood prepared with the celebrity chef's California flair. The open kitchens and splashy decor enhance the energy level. Tip: the downstairs cafe is less expensive, and the food is just as tasty.

LAKE BUENA VISTA

Arthur's 27 $$$ *Wyndham Palace Resort, 1900 Lake Buena Vista Drive, tel: (407) 827-3450.* The food is just slightly less spectacular than the view at this elegant, 27th-floor restaurant, featuring expertly prepared Continental cuisine. Ask to be seated in time for the fireworks at Disney World. Reservations required.

Hemingways $$–$$$ *Hyatt Regency Grand Cypress Resort, 1 Grand Cypress Boulevard, tel: (407) 239-1234.* Lobster, crab cakes, steaks, and a variety of game are just a few of the hearty entrees served at this inviting shrine to Ernest Hemingway and the Key West ambiance he loved so well. The restaurant overlooks the hotel's huge pool, with views of (simulated) waterfalls, streams, and a beach.

Pebbles $$ *12551 State Road 535 at Crossroads, tel: (407) 827-1111.* California cuisine meets Florida ingredients at this contemporary eatery, popular with a young, hip crowd. Try the salmon sautéed with artichoke hearts or the Florida citrus chicken with pecan cous-cous. Four other locations in the Orlando area attest to the restaurant's successful formula of creative dishes at moderate prices.

Columbia $ *649 Front Street, Celebration, tel: (407) 566-1505.* Housed in what looks like an old Spanish palace, this branch of the famous Tampa restaurant serves paella, chicken Valenciana (baked with yellow rice and smoked ham), red snapper Alicante (a savory seafood casserole), *ropa vieja* (spicy shredded beef), and other Spanish and Cuban specialties.

UNIVERSAL ORLANDO

Delfino Riviera $$$$ *Portofino Bay Hotel, tel: (407) 503-3463.* Artfully prepared Ligurian cuisine is the bill of fare at this roman-tic ristorante overlooking the harbor at Universal's premier hotel. Grilled meats redolent of rosemary and fennel are usually on the menu, as are several excellent pasta choices. Seafood dishes are especially subtle (a rarity in this town), with such recent high-lights as sea bass *polpette* (fritters, more or less), lobster risotto, and tuna carpaccio. Sky-high prices, but an experience worth splurging on.

Emeril's Restaurant Orlando $$$$ *CityWalk, tel: (407) 224-2424.* CityWalk's finest and most expensive restaurant features the culinary creations of television chef Emeril Lagasse. As-sertive Creole flavors bubble up through specialties like pork chops with caramelized sweet potatoes and grilled fish over open-faced ravioli. Wine connoisseurs can choose from more than 10,000 bottles. The desserts are equally glorious, transform-ing homey favorites like root beer floats and banana cream pie into decadent masterpieces. If possible, make reservations sever-al weeks in advance.

Hard Rock Cafe $–$$ *CityWalk, tel: (407) 351-7625.* As they say in the restaurant biz, you can't eat atmosphere. Still, it's hard to concentrate on food when there's so much cool stuff to look at.

Here at the world's largest Hard Rock Cafe, a pink Cadillac revolves over the bar; a mural of dead rock stars adorns the ceiling; and the walls are plastered with instruments that have been strummed and drummed by some of the heaviest hitters in rock. Though the food is almost besides the point, the kitchen does a creditable job with tried-and-true American fare – humongous sandwiches and hamburgers, barbecued ribs, pot roast, T-bone steak.

Latin Quarter $$$ *CityWalk, tel: (407) 224-9255*. Both food and music are spicy at the Latin Quarter, dedicated to the culture and cuisine of 21 Latin American nations. Diners tuck into platters of *milhojas tostones con cangrejo* (fried plantains with crab-meat), *puerco asado* (roasted pork), paella, and other *nuevo latino* creations, while a mariachi band wanders among the tables. After dinner, a 13-piece orchestra and professional dance troupe take the stage.

Mythos $$ *Islands of Adventure, tel: (407) 224-4534*. Ensconced within a regally appointed 'cavern' is the park's finest restaurant. The menu changes often, but travelers accustomed to mediocre theme-park food will be delighted by such ambitious entrees as wood-roasted lobster, cedar-planked salmon, and wood-fired pizza. The list of American wines isn't vast but is carefully chosen.

The Palm $$$ *Hard Rock Hotel, 5800 Universal Boulevard, tel: (407) 503-7256*. Carnivores can slice into slabs of beef at this knock-off of the famous New York steakhouse – a favorite with the meat and martini crowd. Like the original, there are celebrity cari-catures on the wall and a whiff of testosterone in the air. Poultry, lobster, and pasta are also on the menu.

Pastamoré $–$$ *CityWalk, tel: (407) 224-2244*. There's neither a theme nor a celebrity attached to Pastamoré, a capacious Italian restaurant with an attractive contemporary atmosphere, serving up abundant portions of eggplant parmigiana, veal Marsala, and at least a dozen varieties of pizza and pasta. An option to dine family-style let's you taste a little bit of everything, including the *dolci assortiti*, a selection of yummy desserts.

INTERNATIONAL DRIVE

Bahama Breeze $ *8849 International Drive, tel: (407) 248-2499.* A tropical party atmosphere prevails at this popular restaurant, where chefs laboring in an open kitchen serve up Caribbean standbys such as coconut curry chicken, paella, and jerk chicken with a contemporary twist. Expect a long wait to be seated, even with reservations.

Cafe Tu Tu Tango $ *8625 International Drive, tel: (407) 248-2222.* Painters work on canvases while you dine on small, *tapas*-style dishes at this artsy restaurant, where the work of local artists crowds the walls, and musicians, dancers, and other performers occasionally wander among the tables.

Capriccio $ *Peabody Hotel, 9801 International Drive, tel: (407) 352-4000.* A show kitchen is the center of attention at this upscale, marble-clad restaurant specializing in gourmet pizza, grilled meats and seafood, heaping bowls of pasta, and other Italian dishes.

Ming Court $ *9188 International Drive, tel: (407) 351-9988.* Interior koi ponds and gardens set the stage at this fine Chinese restaurant. The chefs cook up specialties of several provinces, as well as a delectable dim sum menu. Ask for a table near the open kitchen.

Race Rock $ *8986 International Drive, tel: (407) 248-9876.* Race fans will be in hog heaven at this motorsports restaurant packed with stock cars, dragsters, and motorcycles. Overstuffed sandwiches, burgers, ribs, pasta, pizza, and several fancier entrees are on the menu.

DOWNTOWN ORLANDO

Boheme Restaurant $$$ *325 South Orange Avenue, tel: (407) 313-9000.* A sumptuous art-filled dining room in the Westin Grand Bohemian Hotel sets the stage for sophisticated Continental dishes and an extensive choice of wines. The menu changes often, but highlights include jumbo 'peeky toe' crab cake, asparagus-crusted scallops, and pepper-seared Angus carpaccio. The cognac lobster bisque is especially noteworthy. The Sunday jazz brunch is not to be missed.

El Bohio Cafe $ *5756 Dahlia Drive, tel: (407) 282-1723*. Some of the best Cuban cuisine in the area, including sweet fried plantains, flan, and stuffed yuca. *Ropa vieja* is a traditional favorite.

Harvey's Bistro $$ *390 North Orlando Avenue, tel: (407) 246-6560*. A little European style goes a long way at this bistro popular with business lunchers and nighttime revelers. Even humble pot roast is transformed into something special, not to mention more ambitious choices such as seared calf liver, crab cakes, and roasted duck.

Le Provence $$–$$$ *50 East Pine Street, tel: (407) 843-1320*. French cuisine is the attraction at this contemporary bistro, to which locals come for grilled lobster with saffron cream sauce, smoked quail, basil-crusted lamb, and other interpretations of classic dishes. The prix-fixe menu is a pretty good deal.

Little Saigon $ *1106 East Colonial Drive, tel: (407) 423-8539*. This no-nonsense family-run restaurant is a welcome addition to a town that celebrates simulation over authenticity. Traditional Vietnamese dishes range from delicate spring rolls and rice noodles to big bowls of soup and fiery stir fries.

Manuel's on the 28th $$$–$$$$ *390 North Orange Avenue, tel: (407) 246-6580*. Stunning views accompany your meal at this elegant restaurant on the 28th floor of the Bank of America building. Equally dazzling are the artfully presented entrées – asparagus-speared ahi tuna, phyllo-wrapped lamb loin, filet mignon with smoked gouda potatoes, and more. An impressive setting for an impressive meal.

White Wolf Cafe $ *829 North Orange Avenue, tel: (407) 895-9911*. This tiny slice of Bohemia is a breath of fresh air in theme-crazed Orlando. The service isn't exactly snappy, but the atmosphere is friendly and the menu – ranging from egg salad sandwiches to wild mushroom lasagna – has enough creative quirks to sustain your interest.

INDEX

The world's largest collection of visual travel guides

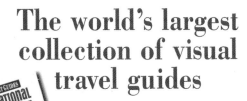

Insight Guides provide the complete
...nd,
...rage

**Ins...
author's ...
best thi...
T...

...acked
...nce
...nt
sights are cross-referenced to the maps

Berlitz Pocket Guides put the world
in your pocket with detailed information,
an easy-to-use A–Z of practical advice,
eye-catching photography and clear maps

(A p a   P u b l i c a t i o n s)